Grang P9-DUH-281

O FOR A BOOKE

O for a Booke and a shadie nooke,
*   Eyther in-a-doore or out ;*
With the grene leaves whispering overhede,
*   Or the Streete cryes all about*
Where I maie Reade all at my ease,
*   Both of the Newe and Olde ;*
For a jollie goode Booke whereon to looke
*   Is better to me than Golde.*

The Second Daffodil Poetry Book

Compiled by Ethel L. Fowler

Granger Index Reprint Series

BOOKS FOR LIBRARIES PRESS
FREEPORT, NEW YORK

First Published 1931

Reprinted 1970 by arrangement with
Sidgwick & Jackson, Ltd.

INTERNATIONAL STANDARD BOOK NUMBER:
0-8369-6177-3

LIBRARY OF CONGRESS CATALOG CARD NUMBER:
75-123389

PRINTED IN THE UNITED STATES OF AMERICA

PREFACE

THIS Second Daffodil Poetry Book is the result of twenty years of experience—with all their ups and downs—in teaching English poetry to English young people between the ages of eleven and sixteen.

However sympathetic, however docile the teacher may be, he can never fathom fully the likes and dislikes of youth ; but he can progress in the hard task of learning how to satisfy the normal desire of the normal individual for beauty of form, beauty of sound, beauty of content.

I know that many, no, most of these poems have satisfied such a craving—a craving none the less real for being an inarticulate one.

E. L. FOWLER, B.A.
*Senior English Mistress, Ipswich
Municipal Secondary School for Girls.*

INDEX OF AUTHORS

₊ *Authors, their representatives, and Publishers, to whom the Compiler desires to make grateful acknowledgements for permission to use copyright poems, are named in parentheses after the Author's name.*

THE SECOND
DAFFODIL POETRY BOOK

PART I

1. DAFFADOWNDILLY

G ROWING in the vale
　　By the uplands hilly,
Growing straight and frail,
　　Lady Daffadowndilly.

In a golden crown,
And a scant green gown,
　　While the spring blows chilly,
Lady Daffadown,
　　Sweet Daffadowndilly.

Christina Rossetti.

2. FLOWERS O' THE SPRING

O PROSERPINA,
　　For the flowers now, that, frighted, thou lett'st
fall
From Dis's waggon ! daffodils,
That come before the swallow dares, and take
The winds of March with beauty ; violets, dim,
But sweeter than the lids of Juno's eyes

Or Cytherea's breath ; pale primroses,
That die unmarried, ere they can behold
Bright Phœbus in his strength . . . bold oxlips, and
The crown-imperial ; lilies of all kinds,
The flower-de-luce being one !   O, these I lack,
To make you garlands of.

William Shakespeare.
(from *The Winter's Tale.*)

3. SNOWDROP

Many, many welcomes,
    February fair-maid,
Ever as of old time,
    Solitary firstling,
Coming in the cold time,
Prophet of the gay time,
Prophet of the May time,
Prophet of the roses,
Many, many welcomes,
    February fair-maid !

Alfred Lord Tennyson.

4. THE CELANDINE

Pansies, Lilies, King-cups, Daisies,
    Let them live upon their praises ;
There's a flower that shall be mine,
'Tis the little Celandine !
Ere a leaf is on a bush,
In the time before the thrush

Has a thought about its nest,
   Thou wilt come with half a call,
Spreading out thy glossy breast,
   Like a careless prodigal ;
Telling tales about the sun,
When we've little warmth or none.

Careless of thy neighbourhood,
   Thou dost show thy pleasant face ;
On the moor or in the wood,
   In the lane—there's not a place,
Howsoever mean it be,
But 'tis good enough for thee.
                William Wordsworth.

5. FEBRUARY

THE robin on my lawn
   He was the first to tell
How in the frozen dawn,
   This miracle befell—
Waking the meadows white
   With hoar, the iron road
Agleam with splintered light,
   And ice where water flowed :
Till, when the low sun drank
   Those milky mists that cloak
Hanger and hollied bank,
   The winter world awoke
To hear the feeble bleat
   Of lambs on the downland farms ;
A blackbird whistled sweet ;
   Old beeches moved their arms

Into a mellow haze
Aerial, newly-born :
And I, alone, agaze,
Stood waiting for the thorn
To break in blossoms white,
Or burst in a green flame—
So, in a single night,
Fair February came,
Bidding my lips to sing
Or whisper their surprise,
With all the joys of spring
And morning in her eyes.

Francis Brett Young.

6. MARCH

I BLOW an arouse
   Through the world's wide house
To quicken the torpid earth :
Grappling, I fling
Each feeble thing,
But bring strong life to the birth.
I wrestle and frown
And topple down :
I wrench, I rend, I uproot :
Yet the violet
Is born where I set
The sole of my flying foot.
And in my wake
Frail wind-flowers quake,
And the catkins promise fruit.

I drive ocean ashore
With rush and roar,
And he cannot say me nay.
My harpstrings all
Are the forests tall,
Making music when I play.
And as others perforce,
So I on my course
Run, and needs must run,
With sap on the mount,
And buds past count,
And rivers and clouds and sun ;
With seasons and breath,
And time and death,
And all that has yet begun.

Christina Rossetti.

7. THE PIPER

PIPING down the valleys wild,
  Piping songs of pleasant glee,
On a cloud I saw a child
  And he laughing said to me :

" Pipe a song about a Lamb ! "
  So I piped with merry cheer.
" Piper, pipe that song again ; "
  So I piped : he wept to hear.

" Drop thy pipe, thy happy pipe ;
  Sing thy songs of happy cheer ; "
So I sang the same again,
  While he wept with joy to hear.

" Piper, sit thee down and write
    In a book that all may read."
So he vanished from my sight,
    And I plucked a hollow reed,

And I made a rural pen,
    And I stain'd the water clear,
And I wrote my happy songs
    Every child may joy to hear.
                              William Blake.

8. BIRD-SONGS

WHAT bird so sings, yet does so wail ?
    O ! 'tis the ravished nightingale.
" Jug, jug, jug, jug, tereu," she cries,
And still her woes at midnight rise.
Brave prick-song !   Who is't now we hear ?
None but the lark so shrill and clear ;
Now at heaven's gate she claps her wings,
The morn not waking till she sings.
Hark, hark, with what a pretty throat
Poor robin redbreast tunes his note !
Hark how the jolly cuckoos sing,
" Cuckoo," to welcome in the spring !
" Cuckoo," to welcome in the spring !
                              John Lyly.

9. LARKS

WHAT voice of gladness, hark !
    In heaven is ringing ?
From the sad fields the lark
    Is upward winging.

High through the mournful mist that blots our day,
Their songs betray them soaring in the grey.
See them! Nay, they
In sunlight swim; above the furthest stain
Of cloud attain; their hearts in music rain
Upon the plain.

Sweet birds, far out of sight,
Your songs of pleasure
Dome us with joy as bright
As heaven's best azure.

Robert Bridges.

10. HARK! HARK! THE LARK

HARK! hark! the lark at Heaven's gate sings,
And Phœbus 'gins arise,
His steeds to water at those springs
On chaliced flowers that lies;
And winking Mary-buds begin
To ope their golden eyes:
With everything that pretty is,
My lady sweet, arise:
Arise, arise.

William Shakespeare.

11. BY AVON STREAM

THE jonquils bloom round Samarcand—
Maybe; but lulled by Avon stream,
By hawthorn-scented breezes fanned,
'Twere mere perversity to dream
Of Samarcand.

A very heaven the Javan isle !—
   Fond fancy, whither wilt thou stray ?
While bluest skies benignant smile
   On Avon meads, why prate to-day
      Of Javan's isle ?

The bulbul plains by Omar's shrine—
   But still I hold, and ever must,
Lark's tirra-lirra more divine,
   And Stratford Church guards dearer dust
      Than Omar's shrine.

             Arthur Henry Bullen.

12. EASTER

I GOT me flowers to straw Thy way,
   I got me boughs off many a tree ;
But Thou wast up by break of day,
And brought'st Thy sweets along with Thee.

The sun arising in the East,
Though he give light and th' East perfume,
If they should offer to contest
With Thy arising, they presume.

Can there be any day but this,
Though many suns to shine endeavour ?
We count three hundred, but we miss :
There is but one and that one ever.

             George Herbert.

13. SPRING GOETH ALL IN WHITE

SPRING goeth all in white,
    Crowned with milk-white May ;
In fleecy flocks of light
    O'er heaven the white clouds stray.

White butterflies in the air ;
    White daisies prank the ground :
The cherry and hoary pear
    Scatter their snow around.

Robert Bridges.

14. LADY LABURNUM

LABURNUM'S a lady, the Lilac's her lover,
    She promised to meet him, she vowed to be
    there ;
But first she must go for green gloves to her glover,
And next she must comb the gold curls of her hair,
And twirl them all twisty and smooth on her fingers,
And hook her silk bodice and draw her dress straight ;
On, on at her mirror she lingers and lingers :—
Laburnum's a lady who always is late.

The Lilac's her lover, her lover is ready,
He's splendid in purple, fine linen and lace,
His kerchief is perfumed, he looks for his lady
His lady still looks in the glass at her face.

He fumes and he frets in regret and amazement,
She promised to meet him and here is the date ;
He sees but a glimpse of gold curls at her casement :—
Laburnum's a lady who always is late.

He waits in the sun till his purple has faded,
He waits in the wind till the perfume has died,
The ruffles are dusty, the lover is jaded
Ere out comes Laburnum at length in her pride.
Her keys in her pocket, her curls long and shining,
She comes to her lover, he droops at the gate,
With splendour half gone and with glory declining :—
Laburnum's a lady who always is late.

Then weep for the fate of them, Lilac-Laburnum,
Who decked themselves out for each other so fine,
Each hoping for praises that now cannot earn 'em,
For lone in her beauty she too shall decline.
Her flounces shall fray, and her curls shall grow
       shorter ;
Write over her tomb, with a tear for her fate,
" She kept her love waiting three days and a quarter,
Laburnum, a lady who always was late."

                              ffrida Wolfe.

15. SUMMER

G LOW-WORMS like the daisies peer ;
       Roses in the thickets fade,
Grudging every petal dear ;
Swinging incense in the shade,
The honeysuckle's chandelier
Twinkles down a shadowy glade.

Now is Nature's restful mood :
Death-still stands the sombre fir ;
Hardly where the rushes brood
Something crawling makes a stir ;
Hardly in the underwood
Russet pinions softly whirr.

John Davidson.

16. MIDSUMMER

Soon will the high Midsummer pomps come on,
  Soon will the musk carnations break and swell,
Soon shall we have gold-dusted snapdragon,
  Sweet-William with his homely cottage smell,
  And stocks in fragrant blow ;
Roses that down the alleys shine afar,
  And open jasmine-muffled lattices,
  And groups under the dreaming garden trees,
And the full-moon, and the white evening-star.

Matthew Arnold (from " *Thyrsis* ").

17. SOMER

Now welcome somer, with thy sonnë softe
  That hast this wintrës weders over-shake,
And driven away the longë nightës blake !

Seynt Valentyn, that art full hy on lofte,
Thus singen smalë foulës for thy sake,
" Now welcome somer, with thy sonnë softe
That hast this wintrës weders over-shake."

Wel han they causë for to gladen ofte
Sith ech of hem recoverëd hath his make ;
Ful blisful may they singen when they wake,

" Now welcome somer, with thy sonnë softe
That hath this wintrës weders over-shake,
And driven away the longë nightës blake."

Geoffrey Chaucer.

18. SONG

How sweet I roamed from field to field,
   And tasted all the summer's pride,
Till I the Prince of Love beheld
   Who in the sunny beams did glide.

He showed me lilies for my hair,
   And blushing roses for my brow ;
He led me through his gardens fair
   Where all his golden pleasures grow.

With sweet May-dews my wings were wet,
   And Phœbus fired my vocal rage ;
He caught me in his silken net,
   And shut me in his golden cage.

He loves to sit and hear me sing,
   Then, laughing, sports and plays with me ;
Then stretches out my golden wing,
   And mocks my loss of liberty.

William Blake.

19. THE RAIN

I HEAR leaves drinking rain ;
   I hear rich leaves on top
Giving the poor beneath
   Drop after drop ;
'Tis a sweet noise to hear
These green leaves drinking near.

And when the Sun comes out,
   After this rain shall stop,
A wondrous light will fill
   Each dark, round drop ;
I hope the Sun shines bright ;
'Twill be a lovely sight.

William H. Davies.

20. LISTENING TO THE WIND

GOD is at the Organ !
   I can hear
A mighty music
Echoing, far and near.

God is at the Organ !
And its keys
Are rolling waters, storm-strewn moorlands,
Trees.

God is at the Organ !
I can hear
A mighty music
Echoing, far and near.

Egbert Sandford.

21. THE WIND

Who has seen the wind ?
  Neither I nor you ;
But when the leaves hang trembling,
  The wind is passing through.

Who has seen the wind ?
  Neither you nor I ;
But when the trees bow down their heads,
  The wind is passing by.

O Wind, why do you never rest,
  Wandering whistling to and fro,
Bringing rain out of the west,
  From the dim north bringing snow ?

Christina Rossetti.

22. AUTUMN

Thou comest, Autumn, heralded by the rain,
  With banners, by great gales incessant fanned,
Brighter than brightest silks of Samarcand,
And stately oxen harnessed to thy wain !
Thou standest, like imperial Charlemagne,
Upon thy bridge of gold ; thy royal hand
Outstretched with benedictions o'er the land,
Blessing the farms throughout thy vast domain !
Thy shield is the red harvest moon, suspended
So long beneath the heaven's o'erhanging eaves ;

Thy steps are by the farmer's prayers attended ;
Like flames upon an altar shine the sheaves ;
And, following thee, in thy ovation splendid,
Thine almoner, the wind, scatters the golden leaves !
Henry Wadsworth Longfellow.

23. WINTER RAIN

EVERY valley drinks,
 Every dell and hollow ;
When the kind rain sinks and sinks,
 Green of Spring will follow.

Yet a lapse of weeks
 Buds will burst their edges,
Strip their wool-coats, glue-coats, streaks,
 In the woods and hedges ;

Weave a bower of love
 For birds to meet each other,
Weave a canopy above
 Nest and egg and mother.

But for fattening rain
 We should have no flowers,
Never a bud or leaf again
 But for soaking showers ;

Never a mated bird
 In the rocking tree-tops,
Never indeed a flock or herd
 To graze upon the lea-crops.

Lambs so woolly white,
  Sheep the sun-bright leas on,
They could have no grass to bite
  But for rain in season :

We should find no moss
  In the shadiest places,
Find no waving meadow-grass
  Pied with broad-eyed daisies.

But miles of barren sand,
  With never a son or daughter ;
Not a lily on the land,
  Or lily on the water.

Christina Rossetti.

24. WINTER

In rigorous hours, when down the iron lane
  The redbreast looks in vain
For hips and haws,
Lo, shining flowers upon my window-pane
The silver pencil of the winter draws.

When all the snowy hill
And the bare woods are still ;
When snipes are silent in the frozen bogs,
And all the garden garth is whelmed in mire,
Lo, by the hearth, the laughter of the logs,
More fair than roses, lo, the flowers of fire !

Robert Louis Stevenson.

25. THE WEAVER OF SNOW

IN Polar noons when the moonshine glimmers,
     And the frost-fans whirl,
And whiter than moonlight the ice-flowers grow,
And the lunar rainbow quivers and shimmers,
And the Silent Laughers dance to and fro,
     A stooping girl
     As pale as pearl
Gathers the frost flowers where they blow :
And the fleet-foot fairies smile, for they know
     The Weaver of Snow.

And she climbs at last to a berg set free,
     That drifteth slow :
And she sails to the edge of the world we see ;
And waits till the wings of the north wind lean
Like an eagle's wings o'er a lochan of green,
     And the pale stars glow
     On berg and floe. . . .
Then down on our world with a wild laugh of glee
She empties her lap full of shimmer and sheen.
And that is the way in a dream I have seen
     The Weaver of Snow.
          " *Fiona Macleod* " (*William Sharp*).

2

26. CHRISTUS NATUS EST

(The author connects his poem with an old church in Essex, on the walls of which, Cock, Duck, Raven, Bull, Lamb, are depicted questioning and answering as in this poem.)

" CHRISTUS natus est," the Cock
        Croweth to the lazy clock.
" Christus natus est," he crows ;
" Christus "—and the Raven knows,
And the Lambs, as you shall hear.
Loudly croweth Chanticleer
With an eager piercing sound
To the Beasts that lie around ;
And they question and reply
While the Sun mounts up the sky.
" Quando ?   Quando ? " and again—
That's the Duck, who's asking *when* ?
" In hac nocte," the Raven croaks
From the old snow-laden oaks.
" Quando ?   Quando ? " from beyond
The willows by the frozen pond.
" In hac nocte," croaks the Raven
From its bare winter's haven.
" Ubi ?   Ubi ? " listen there—
That's the Bull who's asking *where* ?
" In Bethlehem," the Lambs do bleat,
And seek their dams with happy feet.
" Ubi ?   Ubi ? " the Bull lows,
Standing black against the snows ;
And the Lambs " In Bethlehem " :
It was God who told it them.

                    John Alexander Chapman.

27. THE COCK THAT IS THE TRUMPET TO THE MORN

Some say that ever 'gainst that season comes
  Wherein our Saviour's birth is celebrated,
The bird of dawning singeth all night long :
And then, they say, no spirit dare stir abroad ;
The nights are wholesome ; then no planets strike,
No fairy takes, nor witch hath power to charm ;
So hallow'd and so gracious is the time.

William Shakespeare.

28. A CHRISTMAS CAROL

Before the paling of the stars,
  Before the winter morn,
Before the earliest cockcrow,
  Jesus Christ was born :
Born in a stable,
  Cradled in a manger,
In the world His hands had made
  Born a stranger.

Priest and king lay fast asleep
  In Jerusalem,
Young and old lay fast asleep
  In crowded Bethlehem :
Saint and Angel, ox and ass,
  Kept a watch together,
Before the Christmas daybreak
  In the winter weather.

Jesus on His Mother's breast,
   In the stable cold,
Spotless Lamb of God was He,
   Shepherd of the fold :
Let us kneel with Mary maid,
   With Joseph, bent and hoary,
With Saint and Angel, ox and ass,
   To hail the King of Glory.

Christina Rossetti.

29. THE STAR SONG: A CAROL TO THE KING

TELL us, thou clear and heavenly tongue,
   Where is the Babe but lately sprung ?
Lies He the lily-banks among ?

Or say, if this new Birth of ours
Sleeps, laid within some ark of flowers,
Spangled with dew-light ; thou canst clear
All doubts, and manifest the where.

Declare to us, bright star, if we shall seek
Him in the morning's blushing cheek,
Or search the bed of spices through
To find Him out ?

Star

No, this you need not do ;
But only come and see Him rest,
A princely Babe, in's mother's breast.

Chorus

He's seen !   He's seen !   Why then around
Let's kiss the sweet and holy ground ;
And all rejoice, that we have found
A King before conception crown'd.

Come then, come then, and let us bring
Unto our pretty Twelfth-Tide King
Each one his several offering ;

Chorus

And when night comes we'll give Him wassailing :
And that His treble honours may be seen,
We'll choose Him King, and make His Mother Queen
                                            Robert Herrick.

30. A CRADLE SONG

O MEN from the fields !
         Come gently within.
Tread softly, softly,
O men coming in !

Mavourneen is going
From me and from you,
Where Mary will fold him
With mantle of blue.

From reek of the smoke
And cold of the floor,
And the peering of things
Across the half-door.

O men from the fields !
Soft, softly come thro'.
Mary puts round him
Her mantle of blue.

Padraic Colum.

31. NOD

SOFTLY along the road of evening,
    In a twilight dim with rose,
Wrinkled with age, and drenched with dew,
    Old Nod, the shepherd, goes.

His drowsy flock streams on before him,
    Their fleeces charged with gold,
To where the sun's last beam leans low
    On Nod the shepherd's fold.

The hedge is quick and green with briar,
    From their sand the conies creep ;
And all the birds that fly in heaven
    Flock singing home to sleep.

His lambs outnumber a noon's roses,
    Yet, when night's shadows fall,
His blind old sheep-dog, Slumber-soon,
    Misses not one of all.

His are the quiet steeps of dreamland,
    The waters of no more pain,
His ram's bell rings 'neath an arch of stars,
    ' Rest, rest, and rest again.'

Walter de la Mare.

32. WANDERERS

WIDE are the meadows of night,
    And daisies are shining there,
Tossing their lovely dews,
Lustrous and fair ;
And through these sweet fields go,
Wanderers amid the stars—
Venus, Mercury, Uranus, Neptune,
Saturn, Jupiter, Mars.

Attired in their silver, they move,
And circling, whisper and say,
Fair are the blossoming meads of delight
Through which we stray.
                        Walter de la Mare.

33. HYMN TO DIANA

QUEEN and huntress, chaste and fair,
    Now the sun is laid to sleep,
Seated in thy silver chair
    State in wonted manner keep :
        Hesperus entreats thy light,
        Goddess excellently bright.

Earth, let not thy envious shade
    Dare itself to interpose ;
Cynthia's shining orb was made
    Heaven to clear when day did close
        Bless us then with wishéd sight,
        Goddess excellently bright.

Lay thy bow of pearl apart,
    And the crystal-shining quiver ;
Give unto the flying hart
    Space to breathe, how short soever :
        Thou that mak'st a day of night,
        Goddess excellently bright.

Ben Jonson.

34. THE RAINBOW

I SAW the lovely arch
    Of Rainbow span the sky,
The gold sun burning
    As the rain swept by.

In bright ringed solitude
    The showery foliage shone
One lovely moment,
    And the Bow was gone.

Walter de la Mare.

35. THE LAND WHERE THE RAINBOW ENDS

" COME sail with me
    O'er the golden sea,
To the land where the rainbow ends ;
Where the rainbow ends
And the great earth bends
To the weight of the starry sky ;
Where tempests die
With a last fierce cry,

And never a wind is wild ;
There's a Mother mild,
With a little child,
Like a Star set on her knee ;
Go bow you down,
Give Him the crown,
'Tis the Lord of the world you see."

G. A. Studdert Kennedy.

36. NEW HOPE FOR SOME: IN THE BODY AND OUT OF IT

(In Celtic mythology the Fairies are not only outcast angels,
but also lonely spirits between two worlds, since they were not
bad enough to find a home in Hell. Insects are their servants.)

WHEN I am no more thought of,
    Though I'm little thought of now,
When nobody will praise me,
    And nobody will bow,
I'll creep into the garden upon my hands and knees
And sing a song of Jesus beneath the currant-trees ;
And each shiny bug and beetle, the earwigs and the
    snails,
Those little outlaw people whom not a tongue bewails,
Those glinty outlaw people who neither laugh nor cry,
Perpetual as the dust-motes, and lonely as the sky,
Will run and tell the Fairies that here's the Voice of
    Pain
To hew a way to Heaven and get them home again,
Will run and tell the Fairies that here's the thing they
    craved,
That nought and nought make twenty, and strangest
    folk are saved,

Will throng upon my shoulders, and swarm across my
    knees.
And crown me King of Magic beneath the currant-
    trees.

Herbert E. Palmer.

37. A DREAM GARDEN

WILL you come one day to see me
    In my House of Dream ?
I'll light the way before you
    With a rainbow gleam.

You'll see the cloud-walled garden
    Where my lilies grow.
And count the sunflowers swaying
    In a golden row.

The south wind blows the rose leaves
    Before the sun,
In a cloud of crimson sweetness
    When day is done.

And the stars come out a-flutter
    Like moths white-winged,
Among my apple branches
    All flame-be-ringed.

Flame-fair the apples shimmer
    And change and glow,
And nowhere but in cloudland
    Such apples grow.

O come and see my garden,
And my House of Dream,
I'll light the way before you
With a rainbow gleam.

Ella Young.

38. CARROWMORE

IT'S a lonely road through bogland to the lake at
Carrowmore,
And a sleeper there lies dreaming where the water
laps the shore ;
Though the moth-wings of the twilight in their
purples are unfurled,
Yet his sleep is filled with music by the masters of
the world.

There's a hand is white as silver that is fondling
with his hair :
There are glimmering feet of sunshine that are
dancing by him there :
And half-open lips of faery that were dyed a faery
red
In their revels where the Hazel Tree its holy clusters
shed.

" Come away," the red lips whisper, " all the world is
weary now ;
'Tis the twilight of the ages and it's time to quit the
plough.
Oh, the very sunlight's weary ere it lightens up the
dew,
And its gold is changed and faded before it falls to
you.

" Though your colleen's heart be tender, a tenderer
  heart is near.
What's the starlight in her glances when the stars
  are shining clear ?
Who would kiss the fading shadow when the flower-
  face glows above ?
'Tis the beauty of all Beauty that is calling for your
  love."

Oh, the great gates of the mountain have opened
  once again,
And the sound of song and dancing falls upon the
  ears of men,
And the Land of Youth lies gleaming, flushed with
  rainbow light and mirth,
And the old enchantment lingers in the honey-heart
  of earth.

A. E.

39. DAWN

THE strange blue light which comes before the morn,
  Steals along the marshy banks forlorn ;

The noises of the night have died away,
There comes the hush that heralds in the day,
  The boat is floating down to Camelot.

A wind sobs low and drifts among the sedge,
A primrose glow lifts the horizon's edge ;

The river laps upon the barge's side,
Bearing it ever downward with the tide,
  The boat is floating down to Camelot.

The trees each side the river bend their head
In tender homage to the silent Dead

And so between the hour of night and day,
The Lily-maid passed down the river way,
  The boat has floated down to Camelot.
                              Lady Alix Egerton.

40. THE LORDLY ONES

How beautiful they are,
    The lordly ones
Who dwell in the hills,
In the hollow hills.

They have faces like flowers,
And their breath is a wind
That blows over summer meadows,
Filled with dewy clover.

Their limbs are more white
Than shafts of moonshine :
They are more fleet
Than the March wind.

They laugh and are glad,
And are terrible :
When their lances shake and glitter
Every green reed quivers.

How beautiful they are,
How beautiful,
The lordly ones
In the hollow hills.
          " Fiona Macleod " (William Sharp).

41. THE SONG OF WANDERING ÆNGUS

I WENT out to the hazel wood,
  Because a fire was in my head,
And cut and peeled a hazel wand,
And hooked a berry to a thread ;
And when white moths were on the wing,
And moth-like stars were flickering out,
I dropped a berry in a stream
And caught a little silver trout.

When I had laid it on the floor
I went to blow the fire aflame,
But something rustled on the floor,
And some one called me by my name ;
It had become a glimmering girl
With apple blossom in her hair
Who called me by my name and ran
And faded through the brightening air.

Though I am old with wandering
Through hollow lands and hilly lands,
I will find out where she has gone,
And kiss her lips and take her hands,
And walk among long dappled grass,
And pluck till time and times are done
The silver apples of the moon,
The golden apples of the sun.

William Butler Yeats.

42. MOONLIT APPLES

AT the top of the house the apples are laid in rows,
And the skylight lets the moonlight in, and
those
Apples are deep-sea apples of green. There goes
A cloud on the moon in the autumn night.

A mouse in the wainscot scratches, and scratches, and
then
There is no sound at the top of the house of men
Or mice; and the cloud is blown, and the moon again
Dapples the apples with deep-sea light.

They are lying in rows there, under the gloomy beams;
On the sagging floor; they gather the silver streams
Out of the moon, those moonlit apples of dreams,
And quiet is the steep stair under.

In the corridors under there is nothing but sleep.
And stiller than ever on orchard boughs they keep
Tryst with the moon, and deep is the silence, deep
On moon-washed apples of wonder.

John Drinkwater.

43. AN OLD WOMAN OF THE ROADS

O! TO have a little house!
To own the hearth and stool and all!
The heaped up sods upon the fire,
The pile of turf against the wall!

To have a clock with weights and chains
And pendulum swinging up and down !
A dresser filled with shining delph,
Speckled and white and blue and brown !

I could be busy all the day
Clearing and sweeping hearth and floor,
And fixing on their shelf again
My white and blue and speckled store !

I could be quiet there at night
Beside the fire and by myself,
Sure of a bed and loth to leave
The ticking clock and the shining delph !

Och ! but I'm weary of mist and dark,
And roads where there's never a house nor bush,
And tired I am of bog and road,
And the crying wind and the lonesome hush !

And I am praying to God on high,
And I am praying Him night and day,
For a little house—a house of my own—
Out of the wind's and rain's way.

                              Padraic Colum.

44. THE HOUSE BY BLAVET

I HAD a house by Blavet,
    Its walls were curds and cream,
Each door-post was a sausage
And a fat eel each beam.

The hearth was made of pancakes,
The roof of gingerbread,
Of honeycomb the windows,
And sugar was the bed.

Hunger one day came on me,
I had no bread nor meat,
I pulled it down and ate it,
My house that was so sweet.

I ate up in my hunger
My house from thatch to floor ;
Homeless I now go begging
For crusts from door to door.

Richard Lawson Gales.

45. TILLIE

OLD Tillie Turveycombe
    Sat to sew,
Just where a patch of fern did grow ;
There, as she yawned,
And yawn wide did she,
Floated some seed
Down her gull-e-t ;
And look you once,
And look you twice,
Poor old Tillie
Was gone in a trice ;
But oh, when the wind
Do a-moaning come,
'Tis poor old Tillie
Sick for home ;

And oh, when a voice
In the mist do sigh,
Old Tillie Turveycombe's
Floating by.

Walter de la Mare.

46. THE FALCON HATH BORNE MY MATE AWAY

LULLY, lulley : lully, lulley !
 The falcon hath borne my mate away !
He bare him up, he bare him down,
He bare him into an orchard brown.
In that orchard there was a hall
That was hanged with purple and pall ;
And in that hall there was a bed,
It was hanged with gold so red ;
And in that bed there lieth a knight,
His wounds bleeding day and night ;
By that bedside kneeleth a may,
And she weepeth both night and day ;
And by that bedside there standeth a stone,
Corpus Christi written thereon.
Lully, lulley, lully, lulley !

Anonymous.

47. THE PHŒNIX

BY feathers green, across Casbeen
 The pilgrims track the Phœnix flown
By gems he strewed in waste and wood,
 And jewelled plumes at random thrown.

Till wandering far, by moon and star,
   They stand beside the fruitful pyre,
Where breaking bright with sanguine light
   The impulsive bird forgets his sire.

Those ashes shine like ruby wine,
   Like bag of Tyrian murex spilt,
The claw, the jowl of the flying fowl
   Are with the glorious anguish gilt.

So rare the light, so rich the sight,
   Those pilgrim men, on profit bent,
Drop hands and eyes and merchandise,
   And are with gazing most content.
                      Arthur Christopher Benson.

48. AN OLD SONG RE-SUNG

I saw a ship a-sailing, a-sailing, a-sailing,
   With emeralds and rubies and sapphires in her
   hold ;
And a bosun in a blue coat bawling at the railing,
   Piping through a silver call that had a chain of gold ;
   The summer wind was failing and the tall ship
   rolled.

I saw a ship a-steering, a-steering, a-steering,
   With roses in red thread worked upon her sails ;
With sacks of purple amethysts, the spoils of buccan-
   eering,
   Skins of musky yellow wine and silk in bales,
   Her merry men were cheering, hauling on the brails.

I saw a ship a-sinking, a-sinking, a-sinking,
  With glittering sea-water splashing on her decks,
With seamen in her spirit-room singing songs and
    drinking,
    Pulling claret bottles down, and knocking off the
    necks,
    The broken glass was chinking as she sank among
    the wrecks.

John Masefield.

49. THE INCHCAPE ROCK

No stir in the air, no stir in the sea,
  The ship was as still as she could be,
Her sails from heaven received no motion,
Her keel was steady in the ocean.

Without either sign or sound of their shock
The waves flow'd over the Inchcape Rock ;
So little they rose, so little they fell,
They did not move the Inchcape Bell.

The good old Abbot of Aberbrothok
Had placed that bell on the Inchcape Rock ;
On a buoy in the storm it floated and swung,
And over the waves its warning rung.

When the Rock was hid by the surges' swell,
The Mariners heard the warning bell ;
And then they knew the perilous Rock,
And blest the Abbot of Aberbrothok.

The sun in heaven was shining gay,
All things were joyful on that day ;
The sea-birds scream'd as they wheel'd round,
And there was joyance in their sound.

The buoy of the Inchcape Bell was seen
A darker speck on the ocean green ;
Sir Ralph the Rover walk'd his deck,
And he fix'd his eye on the darker speck.

He felt the cheering power of spring,
It made him whistle, it made him sing ;
His heart was mirthful to excess,
But the Rover's mirth was wickedness.

His eye was on the Inchcape float ;
Quoth he, ' My men, put out the boat,
And row me to the Inchcape Rock,
And I'll plague the priest of Aberbrothok.'

The boat is lower'd, the boatmen row,
And to the Inchcape Rock they go ;
Sir Ralph bent over from the boat,
And he cut the bell from the Inchcape float.

Down sunk the bell with a gurgling sound,
The bubbles rose and burst around ;
Quoth Sir Ralph, ' The next who comes to the Rock
Won't bless the Abbot of Aberbrothok.'

Sir Ralph the Rover sail'd away,
He scour'd the seas for many a day ;
And now grown rich with plunder'd store,
He steers his course for Scotland's shore.

So thick a haze o'erspreads the sky
They cannot see the sun on high ;
The wind hath blown a gale all day,
At evening it hath died away.

On the deck the Rover takes his stand,
So dark it is they see no land.
Quoth Sir Ralph, ' It will be lighter soon,
For there is the dawn of the rising moon.'

' Canst hear,' said one, ' the breakers roar ?
For methinks we should be near the shore.'
' Now where we are we cannot tell,
But I wish I could hear the Inchcape Bell.'

They hear no sound, the swell is strong ;
Though the wind hath fallen, they drift along,
Till the vessel strikes with a shivering shock :
' O heavens, it is the Inchcape Rock ! '

Sir Ralph the Rover tore his hair,
He curst himself in his despair ;
The waves rush in on every side,
The ship is sinking beneath the tide.

But even now in his dying fear
One dreadful sound could the Rover hear,
A sound as if, with the Inchcape Bell,
The fiends in triumph were ringing his knell.

Robert Southey.

50. SEA-GULLS

WHERE the dark green hollows lift
    Into crests of snow,
Wheeling, flashing, floating by,
White against the stormy sky,
With exultant call and cry
   Swift the sea-gulls go.

Fearless, vagabond and free
   Children of the spray,
Spirits of old mariners
Drifting down the restless years—
Drake's and Hawkins' buccaneers,
   So do seamen say.

Watching, guarding, sailing still
   Round the shores they knew,
Where the cliffs of Devon rise
Red against the sullen skies
(Dearer far than Paradise),
   'Mid the tossing blue.

Not for them the heavenly song ;
  Sweeter still they find
Than those angels, row on row,
Thunder of the bursting snow
Seething on the rocks below,
  Singing of the wind.

Fairer than the streets of gold
  Those wild fields of foam,
Where the horses of the sea
Stamp and whinny ceaselessly,
Warding from all enemy
  Shores they once called home.

So the sea-gulls call and cry
  'Neath the cliffs to-day,
Spirits of old mariners
Drifting down the restless years—
Drake's and Hawkins' buccaneers—
  So do seamen say.

Nora Holland.

51. THE EAGLE

HE clasps the crag with crooked hands ;
  Close to the sun in lonely lands,
Ring'd with the azure world, he stands.

The wrinkled sea beneath him crawls ;
He watches from his mountain walls,
And like a thunderbolt he falls.

Alfred Lord Tennyson.

52. THE EAGLE

THEY have him in a cage
    And little children run
To offer him well-meant bits of bun,
And very common people say, " my word !
Ain't he a 'orrible bird ! "
And the smart, " How absurd !
Poor, captive, draggled, downcast lord of the air ! "

Steadfast in his despair,
He doth not rage ;
But with unconquerable eye
And soul aflame to fly,
Considereth the sun.

T. W. H. Crosland.

53. TIM, AN IRISH TERRIER

IT's wonderful dogs they're breeding now :
    Small as a flea, or large as a cow ;
But my old lad Tim he'll never be bet
By any dog that ever he met,
" Come on," says he, " for I'm not kilt yet."

No matter the size of the dog he'll meet,
Tim trails his coat the length of the street.
D'ye mind his scars an' his ragged ear,
The like of a Dublin Fusilier ?
He's a massacree dog that knows no fear.

But he'd stick to me till his latest breath,
An' he'd go with me to the gates of death.
He'd wait for a thousand years, maybe,
Scratching the door an' whining for me,
If myself were inside in Purgatory.

So I laugh when I hear thim make it plain
That dogs and men never meet again.
For all their talk who'd listen to thim,
With the soul in the shining eyes of him?
Would God be wasting a dog like Tim?

Winifred M. Letts.

54. THE TORTOISESHELL CAT

THE tortoiseshell cat
   She sits on the mat
As gay as a sunflower she;
In orange and black you see her blink,
And her waistcoat's white, and her nose is pink,
And her eyes are green of the sea.
But all is vanity, all the way;
Twilight's coming, and close of day,
And every cat in the twilight's grey,
   Every possible cat.

The tortoiseshell cat
   She is smooth and fat,
And we call her Josephine,
Because she weareth upon her back
This coat of colours, this raven black,
This red of the tangerine.

But all is vanity, all the way ;
Twilight follows the brightest day,
And every cat in the twilight's grey,
    Every possible cat.
              Patrick R. Chalmers.

55. ON THE DEATH OF A FAVOURITE CAT

Drowned in a Tub of Gold Fishes

'TWAS on a lofty vase's side,
    Where China's gayest art had dyed
The azure flowers that blow ;
Demurest of the tabby kind,
The pensive Selima reclined,
    Gazed on the lake below.

Her conscious tail her joy declared ;
The fair round face, the snowy beard,
    The velvet of her paws,
Her coat, that with the tortoise vies,
Her ears of jet, and emerald eyes,
    She saw ; and purred applause.

Still had she gazed ; but midst the tide
Two angel forms were seen to glide,
    The Genii of the stream :
Their scaly armour's Tyrian hue
Thro' richest purple to the view
    Betray'd a golden gleam.

The hapless Nymph with wonder saw :
A whisker first and then a claw,
  With many an ardent wish,
She stretch'd in vain to reach the prize.
What female heart can gold despise ?
  What cat's averse to fish ?

Presumptuous Maid ! with looks intent
Again she stretch'd, again she bent,
  Nor knew the gulf between.
(Malignant Fate sat by, and smiled.)
The slippery verge her feet beguiled,
  She tumbled headlong in.

Eight times emerging from the flood,
She mew'd to ev'ry wat'ry god,
  Some speedy aid to send.
No Dolphin came, no Nereïd stirr'd :
Nor cruel Tom, nor Susan heard.
  A Fav'rite has no friend.

From hence, ye Beauties, undeceived,
Know, one false step is ne'er retrieved,
  And be with caution bold.
Not all that tempts your wand'ring eyes
And heedless hearts, is lawful prize ;
  Nor all that glisters, gold.

                              Thomas Gray.

56. GET UP AND BAR THE DOOR

IT fell about the Martinmas time,
  And a gay time it was then,
When our goodwife got puddings to make,
  And she's boil'd them in the pan.

The wind sae cauld blew south and north,
  And blew into the floor;
Quoth our goodman to our goodwife,
  " Gae out and bar the door."—

" My hand is in my hussyfskep,
  Goodman, as ye may see;
And it should nae be barr'd this hundred year,
  It's no be barr'd for me."

They made a paction 'tween them twa,
  They made it firm and sure,
That the first word whae'er should speak
  Should rise and bar the door.

Then by there came twa gentlemen,
  At twelve o'clock at night,
And they could neither see house nor hall,
  Nor coal nor candle-light,

" Now whether is this a rich man's house,
  Or whether it is a poor? "
But ne'er a word wad ane o' them speak,
  For barring of the door.

And first they ate the white puddings,
    And then they ate the black ;
Though muckle thought the goodwife to hersel',
    Yet ne'er a word she spake.

Then said the ane unto the other,
    " Here, man tak ye my knife ;
Do ye tak off the auld man's beard,
    And I'll kiss the goodwife."—

" But there's nae water in the house,
    And what shall we do than ? "—
" What ails ye at the pudding-broo,
    That boils into the pan ? "

O up and started our goodman,
    An angry man was he :
" Will ye kiss my wife before my een,
    And sca'd me wi' pudding-bree ? "

Then up and started our goodwife,
    Gied three skips on the floor :
" Goodman, you've spoken the foremost word,
    Get up and bar the door ! "

                                    Old Ballad.

57. SONG OF THE CYCLOPS (*Extract*)

Brave iron, brave hammer, from your sound
    The art of music has her ground ;
On the anvil thou keep'st time,
Thy knick-a-knock is a smith's best chime.

Yet thwick-a-thwack, thwick, thwack-a-thwack,
    thwack,
Make our brawny sinews crack.
Then pit-a-pat, pat, pit-a-pat, pat,
Till thickest bars be beaten flat.

We shoe the horses of the sun,
Harness the dragons of the moon ;
Forge Cupid's quiver, bow and arrows,
And our dame's coach that's drawn with sparrows.
Till thwick-a-thwack, thwick, thwack-a-thwack,
    thwack,
Make our brawny sinews crack.
Then pit-a-pat, pat, pit-a-pat, pat,
Till thickest bars be beaten flat.

Jove's roaring cannons and his rammers
We beat out with our Lemnian hammers ;
Mars his gauntlet, helm and spear,
And Gorgon shield are all made here.
Till thwick-a-thwack, thwick, thwack-a-thwack,
    thwack,
Make our brawny sinews crack.
Then pit-a-pat, pat, pit-a-pat, pat,
Till thickest bars be beaten flat.

Venus' kettles, pots and pans
We make, or else she brawls and bans :
Tongs, shovels and irons have their places,
Else she scratches all our faces.

Till   thwick-a-thwack,   thwick,   thwack-a-thwack,
    thwack,
Make our brawny sinews crack,
Then pit-a-pat, pat, pit-a-pat, pat,
Till thickest bars be beaten flat.

Thomas Dekker.

58. THE GREEN GNOME

RING, sing ! ring, sing ! pleasant Sabbath bells !
    Chime, rhyme ! chime, rhyme ! through the
        dales and dells !
Rhyme, ring ! chime, sing ! pleasant Sabbath bells !
Chime, sing ! rhyme, ring ! over fields and fells !

And I gallop'd and I gallop'd on my palfrey white as
    milk,
My robe was of the sea-green woof, my serk was of the
    silk,
My hair was golden yellow, and it floated to my shoe,
My eyes were like two harebells bathed in shining
    drops of dew ;
My palfrey, never stopping, made a music sweetly
    blent
With the leaves of autumn dropping all around me
    as I went ;
And I heard the bells grow fainter, far behind me
    peal and play,
Fainter, fainter, fainter, fainter, till they seem'd to
    die away ;

And beside a silver runnel, on a lonely heap of
  sand,
I saw the green Gnome sitting, with his cheek upon
  his hand ;
Then he started up to see me, and he ran with cry
  and bound,
And drew me from my palfrey white, and set me on
  the ground :
O crimson, crimson were his locks, his face was green
  to see,
But he cried, " O light-hair'd lassie, you are bound
  to marry me ! "
He claspt me round the middle small, he kissed me
  on the cheek,
He kissed me once, he kissed me twice—I could not
  stir or speak ;
He kissed me twice, he kissed me thrice—but when
  he kissed again,
I called aloud upon the name of Him who died for
  men !

Ring, sing ! ring, sing ! pleasant Sabbath bells !
Chime, rhyme ! chime, rhyme ! through the dales
  and dells !
Rhyme, ring ! chime, sing ! pleasant Sabbath bells !
Chime, sing ! rhyme, ring ! over fields and fells !

O faintly, faintly, faintly, calling men and maids to
  pray,
So faintly, faintly, faintly, rang the bells afar
  away ;

4

And as I named the Blessed Name, as in our need
  we can,
The ugly green, green Gnome became a tall and
  comely man !
His hands were white, his beard was gold, his eyes
  were black as sloes,
His tunic was of scarlet woof, and silken were his
  hose ;
A pensive light from Faeryland still linger'd on his
  cheek,
His voice was like the running brook, when he began
  to speak :
" O you have cast away the charm my stepdame put
  on me,
Seven years I dwelt in Faeryland, and you have set
  me free !
O I will mount thy palfrey white, and ride to kirk
  with thee,
And by those sweetly shining eyes, we twain will
  wedded be ! "

.   .   .   .   .

Back we gallop'd, never stopping, he before and I
  behind,
And the autumn leaves were dropping, red and yellow,
  in the wind,
And the sun was shining clearer, and my heart was
  high and proud,
As nearer, nearer, nearer, rang the kirk-bells sweet
  and loud,

And we saw the kirk before us, as we trotted down
    the fells,
And nearer, clearer, o'er us rang the welcome of the
    bells !

Ring, sing ! ring, sing ! pleasant Sabbath bells !
Chime, rhyme ! chime, rhyme ! through the dales
    and dells !
Rhyme, ring ! chime, sing ! pleasant Sabbath bells !
Chime, sing ! rhyme, ring ! over fields and fells !
               Robert Buchanan.

59. ALICE BRAND

I

MERRY it is in the good greenwood,
   When the mavis and merle are singing,
When the deer sweeps by, and the hounds are in cry,
   And the hunter's horn is ringing.

' O Alice Brand, my native land
   Is lost for love of you ;
And we must hold by wood and wold,
   As outlaws wont to do !

' O Alice, 'twas all for thy locks so bright,
   And 'twas all for thine eyes so blue,
That on the night of our luckless flight
   Thy brother bold I slew.

'Now must I teach to hew the beech
  The hand that held the glaive,
For leaves to spread our lowly bed,
  And stakes to fence our cave.

'And for vest of pall, thy fingers small,
  That wont on harp to stray,
A cloak must shear from the slaughter'd deer,
  To keep the cold away.'—

—' O Richard ! if my brother died,
  'Twas but a fatal chance :
For darkling was the battle tried,
  And fortune sped the lance.

'If pall and vair no more I wear,
  Nor thou the crimson sheen,
As warm, we'll say, is the russet grey,
  As gay the forest green.

'And, Richard, if our lot be hard,
  And lost thy native land,
Still Alice has her own Richárd,
  And he his Alice Brand.'

II

'Tis merry, 'tis merry, in good greenwood,
  So blithe Lady Alice is singing ;
On the beech's pride and oak's brown side
  Lord Richard's axe is ringing.

Up spoke the moody Elfin King,
  Who wonn'd within the hill—
Like wind in the porch of a ruin'd church
  His voice was ghostly shrill.

' Why sounds yon stroke on beech and oak,
  Our moonlight circle's screen ?
Or who comes here to chase the deer
  Beloved of our Elfin Queen ?
Or who may dare on wold to wear
  The fairies' fatal green ?

' Up, Urgan, up ! to yon mortal hie,
  For thou wert christen'd man :
For cross or sign thou wilt not fly,
  For mutter'd word or ban.

' Lay on him the curse of the wither'd heart,
  The curse of the sleepless eye ;
Till he wish and pray that his life would part,
  Nor yet find leave to die ! '

III

'Tis merry, 'tis merry, in good greenwood,
  Though the birds have still'd their singing ;
The evening blaze doth Alice raise,
  And Richard is faggots bringing.

Up Urgan starts, that hideous dwarf,
  Before Lord Richard stands,
  And, as he cross'd and bless'd himself,
' I fear not sign,' quoth the grisly elf,
  ' That is made with bloody hands.'

But out then spoke she, Alice Brand,
  That woman void of fear :
' And if there's blood upon his hand,
  'Tis but the blood of deer.'

' Now loud thou liest, thou bold of mood !
  It cleaves unto his hand,
The stain of thine own kindly blood,
  The blood of Ethert Brand.'

Then forward stepp'd she, Alice Brand,
  And made the holy sign :
' And if there's blood on Richard's hand,
  A spotless hand is mine.

' And I conjure thee, Demon elf,
  By Him whom Demons fear,
To show us whence thou art thyself,
  And what thine errand here.'

IV

' 'Tis merry, 'tis merry, in Fairy-land,
  When fairy birds are singing,
When the court doth ride by their monarch's side,
  With bit and bridle ringing :

' And gaily shines the Fairy-land—
   But all is glistening show,
Like the idle gleam that December's beam
   Can dart on ice and snow.

' And fading, like that varied gleam,
   Is our inconstant shape,
Who now like knight and lady seem,
   And now like dwarf and ape.

' It was between the night and day,
   When the Fairy King has power,
That I sunk down in a sinful fray,
And 'twixt life and death was snatch'd away
   To the joyless Elfin bower.

' But wist I of a woman bold
   Who thrice my brow durst sign,
I might regain my mortal mould,
   As fair a form as thine.'

She cross'd him once—she cross'd him twice—
   That lady was so brave ;
The fouler grew his goblin hue,
   The darker grew the cave.

She cross'd him thrice, that lady bold—
   He rose beneath her hand
The fairest knight on Scottish mould,
   Her brother, Ethert Brand !

Merry it is in good green wood,
   When the mavis and merle are singing ;
But merrier were they in Dunfermline grey
   When all the bells were ringing.
Sir Walter Scott (from *The Lady of the Lake*).

60. AS LUCY WENT A-WALKING

As Lucy went a-walking one morning cold and fine,
   There sate three crows upon a bough, and three
times three is nine :
Then ' O ! ' said Lucy, in the snow, ' it's very plain
   to see
A witch has been a-walking in the fields in front of
   me.'

Then stept she light and heedfully across the frozen
   snow,
And plucked a bunch of elder-twigs that near a pool
   did grow :
And, by and by, she comes to seven shadows in one
   place
Stretched black by seven poplar trees against the
   sun's bright face.

She looks to left, she looks to right, and in the midst
   she sees
A little pool of water clear and frozen 'neath the
   trees ;
Then down beside its margent in the crusty snow she
   kneels,
And hears a magic belfry a-ringing with sweet bells.

Clear sang the faint merry peal, then silence on the
    air,
And icy-still the frozen pool and poplars standing
    there :
Then lo ! as Lucy turned her head and looked along
    the snow
She sees a witch—a witch she sees, come frisking to
    and fro.

Her scarlet, buckled shoes they clicked, her heels
    a-twinkling high ;
With mistletoe her steeple hat bobbed as she capered
    by ;
But never a dint, or mark, or print, in the whiteness
    for to see,
Though danced she high, though danced she fast,
    though danced she lissomely.

It seemed 'twas diamonds in the air, or little flakes
    of frost ;
It seemed 'twas golden smoke around, or sunbeams
    lightly tossed ;
It seemed an elfin music like to reeds and warblers
    rose :
' Nay,' Lucy said, ' it is the wind that through the
    branches flows.'

And as she peeps, and as she peeps, 'tis no more one,
    but three,
And eye of bat, and downy wing of owl within the
    tree,

And the bells of that sweet belfry a-pealing as before,
And now it is not three she sees, and now it is not
four.

'O ! who are ye,' sweet Lucy cries, 'that in a
dreadful ring,
All muffled up in brindled shawls, do caper, frisk, and
spring ? '
'A witch, and witches, one and nine,' they straight
to her reply,
And looked upon her narrowly, with green and need-
ling eye.

Then Lucy sees in clouds of gold green cherry trees
upgrow,
And bushes of red roses that bloomed above the
snow ;
She smells, all faint, the almond boughs blowing so
wild and fair,
And doves with milky eyes ascend fluttering in the air.

Clear flowers she sees, like tulip buds, go floating
by like birds,
With wavering tips that warbled sweetly strange
enchanted words ;
And, as with ropes of amethyst, the boughs with
lamps were hung,
And clusters of green emeralds like fruit upon them
clung.

'O witches nine, ye dreadful nine, O witches seven
  and three !
Whence come these wondrous things that I this
  Christmas morning see ? '
But straight, as in a clap, when she of *Christmas* says
  the word,
Here is the snow, and there the sun, but never bloom
  nor bird ;

Nor warbling flame, nor gloaming-rope of amethyst
  there shows,
Nor bunches of green emeralds, nor belfry, well, and
  rose,
Nor cloud of gold, not cherry-tree, nor witch in
  brindled shawl,
But like a dream that vanishes, so vanished were
  they all.

When Lucy sees, and only sees three crows upon a
  bough,
And earthly twigs, and bushes hidden white in driven
  snow,
Then ' O ! ' said Lucy, ' three times three is nine—
  I plainly see
Some witch has been a-walking in the fields in front
  of me.'

Walter de la Mare.

61. ALISON GROSS

O Alison Gross, that lives in yon tower,
    The ugliest witch in the north countrie,
Has trysted me ae day up till her bower,
    And mony fair speeches she made to me.

She straik'd my head an' she kaim'd my hair,
   An' she set me down saftly on her knee ;
Says, " Gin ye will be my lemman sae true,
   Sae mony braw things as I would you gie ! "

She show'd me a mantle o' red scarlet,
   Wi' gouden flowers an' fringes fine ;
Says, " Gin ye will be my lemman sae true,
   This gudely gift it sall be thine."—

" Awa', awa', ye ugly witch,
   Haud far awa', an' let me be !
I never will be your lemman sae true,
   An' I wish I were out o' your company."

She neist brought a sark o' the saftest silk,
   Well wrought wi' pearls about the band ;
Says, " Gin ye will be my lemman sae true,
   This gudely gift ye sall command."

She show'd me a cup o' good red gowd,
   Well set wi' jewels sae fair to see ;
Says, " Gin ye will be my lemman sae true,
   This gudely gift I will you gie."—

" Awa', awa', ye ugly witch,
   Haud far awa', and let me be !
For I wouldna once kiss your ugly mouth
   For a' the gifts that ye could gie."

She turn'd her right an' roun' about,
   And thrice she blaw on a grass-green horn ;
An' she sware by the moon an' the stars abune
   That she'd gar me rue the day I was born.

Then out she has ta'en a silver wand,
   An' she's turn'd her three times roun' and roun' ;
And mutter'd sic words till my strength it fail'd,
   An' I fell down senseless upon the groun'.

She's turn'd me into an ugly worm,
   And gar'd me toddle about the tree ;
And ay, on ilka Saturday night
   My sister Maisry came to me,

Wi' silver bason an' silver kaim,
   To kaim my headie upon her knee ;
But or I had kiss'd wi' Alison Gross
   I'd sooner ha' toddled about the tree.

But as it fell out, on last Hallowe'en,
   When the Seely Court was ridin' by,
The Queen lighted down on a gowany bank
   Nae far from the tree where I wont to lye.

She took me up in her milk-white han',
   An' she's straik'd me three times o'er her knee ;
She changed me again to my proper shape,
   An' nae mair I toddle about the tree.

Old Ballad.

62. THE SLEEPING BEAUTY
I.—THE MAGIC SLEEP

I

YEAR after year unto her feet,
    She lying on her couch alone,
Across the purple coverlet,
    The maiden's jet-black hair has grown,
On either side her tranced form
    Forth streaming from a braid of pearl :
The slumbrous light is rich and warm,
    And moves not on the rounded curl.

II

The silk star-broider'd coverlid
    Unto her limbs itself doth mould,
Languidly ever ; and, amid
    Her full black ringlets downward roll'd,
Glows forth each softly shadow'd arm
    With bracelets of the diamond bright :
Her constant beauty doth inform
    Stillness with love, and day with light.

III

She sleeps : her breathings are not heard
    In palace chambers far apart.
The fragrant tresses are not stirr'd,
    That lie upon her charmed heart.
She sleeps : on either hand upswells
    The gold-fringed pillow lightly press'd :
She sleeps, nor dreams, but ever dwells
    A perfect form in perfect rest.

II.—THE ARRIVAL

I

All precious things, discover'd late,
  To those that seek them issue forth ;
For love in sequel works with fate,
  And draws the veil from hidden worth.
He travels far from other skies—
  His mantle glitters on the rocks—
A fairy prince, with joyful eyes,
  And lighter-footed than the fox.

II

The bodies and the bones of those
  That strove in other days to pass,
Are wither'd in the thorny close,
  Or scatter'd blanching on the grass.
He gazes on the silent dead :
  ' They perish'd in their daring deeds.'
This proverb flashes thro' his head,
  ' The many fail : the one succeeds.'

III

He comes, scarce knowing what he seeks :
  He breaks the hedge : he enters there :
The colour flies into his cheeks :
  He trusts to light on something fair ;
For all his life the charm did talk
  About his path, and hover near
With words of promise in his walk,
  And whisper'd voices at his ear.

IV

More close and close his footsteps wind :
    The Magic Music in his heart
Beats quick and quicker, till he find
    The quiet chamber far apart.
His spirit flutters like a lark,
    He stoops—to kiss her—on his knee.
' Love, if they tresses be so dark,
    How dark those hidden eyes must be ! '

III.—The Revival

I

A touch, a kiss ! the charm was snapt,
    There rose a noise of striking clocks,
And feet that ran, and doors that clapt,
    And barking dogs, and crowing cocks ;
A fuller light illumin'd all,
    A breeze thro' all the garden swept,
A sudden hubbub shook the hall,
    And sixty feet the fountain leapt.

II

The hedge broke in, the banner blew,
    The butler drank, the steward scrawl'd,
The fire shot up, the martin flew,
    The parrot scream'd, the peacock squall'd,
The maid and page renew'd their strife,
    The palace bang'd and buzz'd and clackt,
And all the long-pent stream of life
    Dash'd downward in a cataract.

III

And last with these the king awoke,
    And in his chair himself uprear'd,
And yawn'd, and rubb'd his face, and spoke,
    ' By holy rood, a royal beard !
How say you ? we have slept, my lords.
    My beard has grown into my lap.'
The barons swore, with many words,
    'Twas but an after-dinner's nap.

IV

' Pardy,' return'd the king, ' but still
    My joints are somewhat stiff or so.
My lord, and shall we pass the bill
    I mention'd half an hour ago ? '
The chancellor, sedate and vain,
    In courteous words return'd reply :
But dallied with his golden chain,
    And, smiling, put the question by.

IV.—THE DEPARTURE

I

And on her lover's arm she leant,
    And round her waist she felt it fold,
And far across the hills they went
    In that new world which is the old :
Across the hills, and far away
    Beyond their utmost purple rim,
And deep into the dying day
    The happy princess follow'd him.

5

II

'I'd sleep another hundred years,
  O love, for such another kiss; '
'O wake for ever, love,' she hears,
   'O love, 'twas such as this and this.'
And o'er them many a sliding star,
  And many a merry wind was borne,
And, stream'd thro' many a golden bar,
  The twilight melted into morn.

III

'O eyes long laid in happy sleep!'
  'O happy sleep, that lightly fled!'
'O happy kiss, that woke thy sleep!'
  'O love, thy kiss would wake the dead!'
And o'er them many a flowing range
  Of vapour buoy'd the crescent-bark,
And, rapt thro' many a rosy change,
  The twilight died into the dark.

IV

'A hundred summers! can it be?
  And whither goest thou, tell me where?'
'O seek my father's court with me,
  For there are greater wonders there.'
And o'er the hills, and far away
  Beyond their utmost purple rim,
Beyond the night, across the day,
  Thro' all the world she follow'd him.

Alfred Lord Tennyson
(from *The Day Dream*).

63. EARL MAR'S DAUGHTER

It was intill a pleasant time,
  Upon a summer's day,
The noble Earl Mar's daughter
  Went forth to sport and play.

And as she play'd and sported
  Below a green oak tree,
There she saw a sprightly doo
  Set on a branch so hie.

" O Coo-my-doo, my Love so true,
  If ye'll come down to me,
Ye'll have a cage of good red gold
  Instead o' a simple tree.

" I'll put gold hingers roun' your cage,
  And siller round your wa',
I'll gar ye shine as fair a bird
  As any o' them a'."

And she had not these words well spoke,
  Nor yet these words well said,
Till Coo-my-doo flew from the tower
  And lighted on her head.

Then she has brought this pretty bird
  Hame to her bower and ha',
And made him shine as fair a bird
  As any o' them a'.

When day was gone an' night was come,
　　About the evening-tide,
This lady spied a sprightly youth
　　Stand straight up by her side.

" O, who are ye, young man ? " she said,
　　" What country come ye frae ? "—
" I flew across the sea," he said,
　　" 'Twas but this very day.

" My mither is a queen," he says,
　　" Likewise of magic skill ;
'Twas she that turn'd me to a doo,
　　To fly where'er I will.

" And it was but this very day
　　That I came o'er the sea :
I loved you at a single look ;
　　With you I'll live and dee."—

" O Coo-my-doo, my Love so true,
　　No more from me ye'll gae——"
" That's never my intent, my Love :
　　As ye said, it shall be sae."

Thus he has stay'd in bower with her
　　For twenty years and three ;
Till there came a lord of high renown
　　To court this fair ladye.

But still his proffer she refused,
   And all his presents too ;
Says, " I'm content to live alone
   With my bird Coo-my-doo."

Her father sware a solemn oath,
   Among the nobles all,
" To-morrow, ere I eat or drink,
   That bird I'll surely kill."

The bird was sitting in his cage,
   And heard what he did say ;
He jump'd upon the window-sill :
   " 'Tis time I was away."

Then Coo-my-doo took flight and flew
   Beyond the raging sea,
And lighted at his mother's castle,
   On a tower of gold so hie.

The Queen his mother was walking out,
   To see what she could see,
And there she saw her darling son
   Set on the tower so hie.

" Get dancers here to dance," she said,
   " And minstrels for to play ;
For here's my dear son Florentine
   Come hame wi' me to stay."—

" Instead of dancers to dance, mither,
　　Or minstrels for to play,
Turn four-and-twenty well-wight men
　　Like storks, in feathers gray ;

" My seven sons in seven swans,
　　Above their heads to flee ;
And I myself a gay goshawk,
　　A bird o' high degree."

This flock of birds took flight and flew
　　Beyond the raging sea ;
They landed near the Earl Mar's castle,
　　Took shelter in every tree.

These birds flew up from bush and tree,
　　And lighted on the ha' ;
And when the wedding-train came forth
　　Flew down among them a'.

The storks they seized each wedding guest,
　　That they could not fight or flee ;
The swans they bound the bridegroom fast
　　Unto a green oak tree.

They lighted next on the bride-maidens,
　　Then on the bride's own head ;
And with the twinkling of an e'e,
　　The bride an' them were fled !

There's ancient men at weddings been
   For sixty years or more,
But siccan a curious wedding day
   They never saw before.

For naething could the companie do,
   And naething could they say ;
But they saw a flock o' pretty birds
   That took their bride away.

               Old Ballad.

64. THE FORSAKEN MERMAN

COME, dear children, let us away ;
   Down and away below !
Now my brothers call from the bay ;
Now the great winds shoreward blow ;
Now the salt tides seaward flow ;
Now the wild white horses play,
Champ and chafe and toss in the spray.
Children dear, let us away !
This way, this way !

Call her once before you go—
Call once yet !
In a voice that she will know :
' Margaret ! Margaret ! '
Children's voices should be dear
(Call once more) to a mother's ear :
Children's voices, wild with pain—
Surely she will come again !

Call her once and come away ;
This way, this way.
' Mother dear, we cannot stay !
The wild, white horses foam and fret.'
Margaret ! Margaret !

Come, dear children, come away down ;
Call no more !
One last look at the white-wall'd town,
And the little grey church on the windy shore ;
Then come down.
She will not come though you call all day ;
Come away, come away !

Children dear, was it yesterday
We heard the sweet bells over the bay ?
In the caverns where we lay,
Through the surf and through the swell,
The far-off sound of a silver bell ?
Sand-strewn caverns, cool and deep,
Where the winds are all asleep ;
Where the spent lights quiver and gleam ;
Where the salt weed sways in the stream ;
Where the sea-beasts, ranged all round,
Feed in the ooze of their pasture-ground ;
Where the sea-snakes coil and twine,
Dry their mail and bask in the brine ;
Where great whales come sailing by,
Sail and sail, with unshut eye,
Round the world for ever and aye ?
When did music come this way ?
Children dear, was it yesterday ?

Children dear, was it yesterday
(Call yet once) that she went away?
Once she sate with you and me,
On a red gold throne in the heart of the sea,
And the youngest sate on her knee.
She combed its bright hair, and she tended it well,
When down swung the sound of a far-off bell.
She sighed, she looked up through the clear green sea;
She said: ' I must go, for my kinsfolk pray
In the little grey church on the shore to-day.
'Twill be Easter-time in the world—ah me!
And I lose my poor soul, Merman, here with thee.'
I said: ' Go up, dear heart, through the waves;
Say thy prayer, and come back to the kind sea-caves!'
She smiled, she went up through the surf in the bay,
Children dear, was it yesterday?

Children dear, were we long alone?
' The sea grows stormy, the little ones moan;
Long prayers,' I said, ' in the world they say;
Come!' I said; and we rose through the surf in the
    bay.
We went up the beach, by the sandy down,
Where the sea-stocks bloom, to the white-wall'd
    town;
Through the narrow paved streets, where all was
    still,
To the little grey church on the windy hill.
From the church came a murmur of folk at their
    prayers
But we stood without in the cold blowing airs.

We climb'd on the graves, on the stones worn with
    rains,
And we gazed up the aisle through the small leaded
    panes.

She sate by the pillar ; we saw her clear :
' Margaret, hist ! come quick, we are here !
Dear heart,' I said, ' we are long alone ;
The sea grows stormy, the little ones moan.'
But, ah, she gave me never a look,
For her eyes were sealed to the holy book !
Loud prays the priest ; shut stands the door.
Come away, children, call no more !
Come away, come down, call no more !

Down, down, down,
Down to the depths of the sea !
She sits at her wheel in the humming town,
Singing most joyfully.
Hark, what she sings : ' O joy, O joy,
For the humming street, and the child with its
    toy !
For the priest, and the bell, and the holy well ;
For the wheel where I spun,
And the blessed light of the sun ! '
And so she sings her fill,
Singing most joyfully,
Till the shuttle falls from her hand,
And the whizzing wheel stands still.
She steals to the window, and looks at the sand ;

And over the sand at the sea ;
And her eyes are set in a stare ;
And anon there breaks a sigh,
And anon there drops a tear
From a sorrow-clouded eye,
And a heart sorrow-laden,
A long, long sigh,
For the cold strange eyes of a little Mermaiden
And the gleam of her golden hair.

Come away, away, children ;
Come, children, come down !
The hoarse wind blows colder ;
Lights shine in the town.
She will start from her slumber
When gusts shake the door ;
She will hear the winds howling,
Will hear the waves roar.
We shall see, while above us
The waves roar and whirl,
A ceiling of amber,
A pavement of pearl.
Singing : ' Here came a mortal,
But faithless was she !
And alone dwell for ever
The kings of the sea.'

But, children, at midnight,
When soft the winds blow,
When clear falls the moonlight,
When spring-tides are low,

When sweet airs come seaward
From heaths starr'd with broom,
And high rocks throw mildly
On the blanch'd sands a gloom,
Up the still, glistening beaches,
Up the creeks we will hie,
Over banks of bright seaweed
The ebb-tide leaves dry.
We will gaze, from the sand-hills,
At the white, sleeping town,
At the church on the hill-side—
And then come back down.
Singing : 'There dwells a loved one,
But cruel is she :
She left lonely for ever
The kings of the sea.'

Matthew Arnold.

65. TRUE THOMAS

TRUE Thomas lay on yon grassy bank,
   And he beheld a lady gay,
A lady that was blithe and bold,
   Come riding o'er the ferny brae.

Her skirt was of the grass-green silk,
   Her mantle of the velvet fine,
At each lock of her horse's mane
   Hung fifty silver bells and nine.

True Thomas, he took off his hat,
   And bowed him low down to his knee ;
" All hail, thou mighty Queen of Heaven !
   For thy like on earth I ne'er did see."

" Oh no, oh no, True Thomas," she says,
  " That name does not belong to me ;
I am but the Queen of fair Elfland,
  And I'm come here to visit thee.

" But ye must go with me, Thomas,
  True Thomas, ye must go with me,
For ye must serve me seven years,
  Through weal or woe, as chance may be."

She turned upon her milk-white steed,
  And took true Thomas up behind,
And aye whene'er her bridle rang,
  The steed flew swifter than the wind.

For forty days and forty nights
  He rode through bracken to the knee,
And he saw neither sun nor moon,
  But heard the roaring of the sea.

" Oh, see ye not that bonny road
  Which winds about the ferny brake ?
That is the road to fair Elfland,
  Which thou and I this night must take.

" But Thomas, ye must hold your tongue,
  Whatever ye may hear or see,
For if one word ye should chance to speak,
  Ye'll ne'er get back to your own country."

He has gotten a coat of elfin cloth,
　　And a pair of shoes of velvet green ;
And till seven years were past and gone,
　　True Thomas on earth was never seen.

Old Ballad.

66. KUBLA KHAN

In Xanadu did Kubla Khan
　　A stately pleasure-dome decree :
Where Alph, the sacred river, ran
Through caverns measureless to man
　　Down to a sunless sea.
So twice five miles of fertile ground
With walls and towers were girdled round :
And there were gardens bright with sinuous rills
Where blossom'd many an incense-bearing tree ;
And here were forests ancient as the hills,
Enfolding sunny spots of greenery.

But oh ! that deep romantic chasm which slanted
Down the green hill athwart a cedarn cover !
A savage place ! as holy and enchanted
As e'er beneath a waning moon was haunted
By woman wailing for her demon-lover !
And from this chasm, with ceaseless turmoil seething,
As if this earth in fast thick pants were breathing,

A mighty fountain momently was forced :
Amid whose swift half-intermitted burst

Huge fragments vaulted like rebounding hail,
Or chaffy grain beneath the thresher's flail :
And 'mid these dancing rocks at once and ever
It flung up momently the sacred river.
Five miles meandering with a mazy motion
Through wood and dale the sacred river ran,
Then reach'd the caverns measureless to man,
And sunk in tumult to a lifeless ocean :
And 'mid this tumult Kubla heard from far
Ancestral voices prophesying war !

   The shadow of the dome of pleasure
Floated midway on the waves ;
   Where was heard the mingled measure
From the fountain and the caves.
It was a miracle of rare device,
A sunny pleasure-dome with caves of ice !
A damsel with a dulcimer
In a vision once I saw :
It was an Abyssinian maid,
And on her dulcimer she play'd,
Singing of Mount Abora.
Could I revive within me
Her symphony and song,
To such a deep delight 'twould win me
That with music loud and long,
I would build that dome in air,
That sunny dome ! those caves of ice !
And all who heard should see them there,
And all should cry, Beware ! Beware !
His flashing eyes, his floating hair !

Weave a circle round him thrice,
And close your eyes with holy dread,
For he on honey-dew hath fed,
And drunk the milk of Paradise.

Samuel Taylor Coleridge.

END OF PART I

THE SECOND
DAFFODIL POETRY BOOK

PART II

67. THERE BLOOMS NO BUD IN MAY

THERE blooms no bud in May
   Can for its white compare
With snow at break of day,
   On fields forlorn and bare.

For shadow it hath rose,
   Azure, and amethyst ;
And every air that blows
   Dies out in beauteous mist.

It hangs the frozen bough
   With flowers on which the night
Wheeling her darkness through
   Scatters a starry light.

Fearful of its pale glare
   In flocks the starlings rise ;
Slide through the frosty air,
   And perch with plaintive cries.

Only the inky rook,
    Hunched cold in ruffled wings,
Its snowy nest forsook,
    Caws of unnumbered Springs.

Walter de la Mare.

68. THE SNOWDROP (*Extract*)

THOU first-born of the year's delight,
        Pride of the dewy glade,
In vernal green and virgin white,
        Thy vestal robes, array'd :

'Tis not because thy drooping form
        Sinks graceful on its nest,
When chilly shades from gathering storm
        Affright thy tender breast ;

Nor for yon river islet wild
        Beneath the willow spray,
Where, like the ringlets of a child,
        Thou weav'st thy circle gay ;

'Tis not for these I love thee dear—
        Thy shy averted smiles
To fancy bode a joyous year,
        One of Life's fairy isles.

They twinkle to the wintry moon,
        And cheer th' ungenial day,
And tell us, all will glisten soon
        As green and bright as they.

John Keble.

69. LAST WEEK OF FEBRUARY

Hark to the merry birds, hark how they sing !
  Although 'tis not yet spring
    And keen the air ;
Hale Winter, half resigning ere he go,
  Doth to his heiress show
    His kingdom fair.

In patient russet is his forest spread,
  All bright with bramble red,
    With beechen moss
And holly sheen : the oak silver and stark
  Sunneth his aged bark
    And wrinkled boss.

But 'neath the ruin of the withered brake
  Primroses now awake
    From nursing shades :
The crumpled carpet of the dry leaves brown
  Avails not to keep down
    The hyacinth blades.

The hazel hath put forth his tassels ruffed ;
  The willow's flossy tuft
    Hath slipped him free :
The rose amid her ransacked orange hips
  Braggeth the tender tips
    Of bowers to be.

A black rook stirs the branches here and there,
  Foraging to repair
    His broken home :
And hark, on the ash boughs !   Never thrush did sing
  Louder in praise of Spring,
    When Spring is come.

Robert Bridges.

70. PRAY AND PROSPER

FIRST offer Incense, then thy field and meads
    Shall smile and smell the better by thy beads.
The spangling Dew dredg'd o'er the grass shall be
Turn'd all to Mell, and Manna there for thee.
Butter of Amber, Cream, and Wine and Oil
Shall run as rivers, all throughout thy soil.
Would'st thou to sincere silver turn thy mould ?
Pray once, twice pray ; and turn thy ground to gold.

Robert Herrick.

71. FAREWELL FROST, OR WELCOME THE SPRING (*Extract*)

FLED are the Frosts, and now the Fields appear
    Re-cloth'd in fresh and verdant Diaper.
Thawed are the snows, and now the lusty Spring
Gives to each mead a neat enamelling.
The Palms put forth their Gems, and every Tree
Now swaggers in her leafy gallantry.
The while the Daulian Minstrel sweetly sings,
With warbling notes, her Terean sufferings.

Robert Herrick.

72. WITH A COPY OF HERRICK

FRESH with all airs of woodland brooks
And scents of showers,
Take to your haunt of holy books
This saint of flowers.

When meadows burn with budding May,
And heaven is blue,
Before his shrine our prayers we say,—
Saint Robin true.

Love crowned with thorns is on his staff,—
Thorns of sweet-briar ;
His benediction is a laugh,
Birds are his choir.

His sacred robe of white and red
Unction distils ;
He hath a nimbus round his head
Of daffodils.

Edmund Gosse.

73. DAFFODILS

I WANDERED lonely as a cloud
That floats on high o'er vales and hills,
When all at once I saw a crowd,
A host of golden daffodils ;
Beside the lake, beneath the trees,
Fluttering and dancing in the breeze.

Continuous as the stars that shine
    And twinkle on the milky way,
They stretched in never-ending line
    Along the margin of a bay :
Ten thousand saw I at a glance
Tossing their heads in sprightly dance.

The waves beside them danced, but they
    Outdid the sparkling waves in glee ;
A poet could not but be gay
    In such a jocund company !
I gazed—and gazed—but little thought
What wealth the show to me had brought :

For oft, when on my couch I lie,
    In vacant or in pensive mood,
They flash upon that inward eye
    Which is the bliss of solitude ;
And then my heart with pleasure fills,
And dances with the daffodils.

                      William Wordsworth.

74. HOME THOUGHTS IN LAVENTIE

GREEN gardens in Laventie !
    Soldiers only know the street
Where the mud is churned and splashed about
    By battle-wending feet ;
And yet beside one stricken house there is a glimpse
    of grass,
Look for it when you pass.

Beyond the church whose pitted spire
   Seems balanced on a strand
Of swaying stone and tottering brick,
   Two roofless ruins stand,
And here behind the wreckage where the back wall
     should have been,
We found a garden green.

The grass was never trodden on,
   The little path of gravel
Was overgrown with celandine,
   No other folk did travel
Along its weedy surface, but the nimble-footed mouse
Running from house to house.

So all among the vivid blades
   Of soft and tender grass
We lay, nor heard the limber wheels
   That pass and ever pass
In noisy continuity until their very rattle
Seems in itself a battle.

At length we rose up from this ease
   Of tranquil happy mind,
And searched the garden's little length
   A fresh pleasaunce to find ;
And there some yellow daffodils and jasmine hanging
     high
Did rest the tired eye.

The fairest and most fragrant
   Of the many sweets we found,

Was a little bush of Daphne flower
　Upon a grassy mound,
And so thick were the blossoms set, and so divine
　the scent
That we were well content.

Hungry for Spring, I bent my head,
　The perfume fanned my face,
And all my soul was dancing,
　In that little lovely place,
Dancing with a measured step from wrecked and
　shattered towns
Away . . . upon the Downs.

I saw green banks of daffodil,
　Slim poplars in the breeze,
Great tan-brown hares in gusty March
　A-courting on the leas ;
And meadows with their glittering streams, and
　silver scurrying dace,
Home—what a perfect place !

　　　　　　　　　　　Edward Wyndham Tennant.
BELGIUM, *March* 1916.

75. HOME-THOUGHTS, FROM ABROAD

OH, to be in England
　　Now that April's there,
And whoever wakes in England
Sees, some morning, unaware,
That the lowest boughs and the brushwood sheaf
Round the elm-tree bole are in tiny leaf,
While the chaffinch sings on the orchard bough

In England—now !
And after April, when May follows,
And the whitethroat builds, and all the swallows—
Hark, where my blossom'd pear-tree in the hedge
Leans to the field and scatters on the clover
Blossoms and dewdrops—at the bent spray's edge—
That's the wise thrush ; he sings each song twice over,
Lest you should think he never could recapture
The first fine careless rapture !
And though the fields look rough with hoary dew,
All will be gay when noontide wakes anew
The buttercups, the little children's dower,
—Far brighter than this gaudy melon-flower !

Robert Browning.

76. SONNET ON EASTER

Most glorious Lord of life ! that on this day
    Didst make Thy triumph over death and sin ;
   And having harrowed hell did'st bring away
   Captivity thence captive, us to win ;
This glorious day, dear Lord, with joy begin ;
   And grant that we, for whom Thou diddest die,
   Being with Thy dear blood clean washed from sin,
   May live for ever in felicity ;
And that Thy love we weighing worthily
   May likewise love Thee for the same again ;
   And for Thy sake that all like dear didst buy,
   With love may one another entertain.
So let us love, dear love, like as we ought :
Love is the lesson which the Lord us taught.

Edmund Spenser.

77. SONG ON MAY MORNING

Now the bright morning-star, Day's harbinger,
   Comes dancing from the East, and leads with
      her
The flowery May, who from her green lap throws
The yellow cowslip and the pale primrose.
  Hail, bounteous May, that dost inspire
  Mirth, and youth, and warm desire !
  Woods and groves are of thy dressing ;
  Hill and dale doth boast thy blessing.
Thus we salute thee with our early song,
And welcome thee, and wish thee long.

John Milton.

78. SONG

A sunny shaft did I behold,
   From sky to earth it slanted :
And poised therein a bird so bold—
   Sweet bird, thou wert enchanted !

He sunk, he rose, he twinkled, he trolled
   Within that shaft of sunny mist ;
His eyes of fire, his beak of gold,
   All else of amethyst !

And thus he sang : " Adieu ! adieu !
Love's dreams prove seldom true.
The blossoms they make no delay :
The sparkling dew-drops will not stay.
    Sweet month of May,

We must away ;
   Far, far away !
      To-day ! to-day ! "
           Samuel Taylor Coleridge.

79. TO DAFFODILS

Fair Daffodils, we weep to see
   You haste away so soon :
As yet the early-rising Sun
  Has not attain'd his noon.
     Stay, stay,
  Until the hasting day
     Has run
  But to the even-song ;
And, having pray'd together, we
  Will go with you along.

We have short time to stay, as you,
  We have as short a Spring ;
As quick a growth to meet decay
  As you, or any thing.
     We die,
  As your hours do, and dry
     Away
  Like to the Summer's rain ;
Or as the pearls of morning's dew
  Ne'er to be found again.
           Robert Herrick.

80. TO THE CUCKOO

O BLITHE new-comer! I have heard,
    I hear thee and rejoice :
O Cuckoo! shall I call thee Bird,
    Or but a wandering Voice ?

While I am lying on the grass
    Thy twofold shout I hear ;
From hill to hill it seems to pass,
    At once far off and near.

Though babbling only to the vale
    Of sunshine and of flowers,
Thou bringest unto me a tale
    Of visionary hours.

Thrice welcome, darling of the Spring !
    Even yet thou art to me
No Bird, but an invisible thing,
    A voice, a mystery ;

The same whom in my school-boy days
    I listened to ; that Cry
Which made me look a thousand ways
    In bush, and tree, and sky.

To seek thee did I often rove
    Through woods and on the green ;
And thou wert still a hope, a love ;
    Still longed for, never seen.

And I can listen to thee yet ;
    Can lie upon the plain
And listen, till I do beget
    That golden time again.

O blessed Bird ! the earth we pace
    Again appears to be
An unsubstantial faery place,
    That is fit home for Thee !
                William Wordsworth.

81. TO THE NIGHTINGALE

O NIGHTINGALE, that on yon bloomy spray
    Warblest at eve, when all the woods are still,
Thou with fresh hope the lover's heart dost fill,
While the jolly hours lead on propitious May.
The liquid notes that close the eye of day,
    First heard before the shallow cuckoo's bill,
    Portend success in love.   O, if Jove's will
Have linked that amorous power to thy soft lay,
Now timely sing, ere the rude bird of hate
    Foretell my hopeless doom in some grove nigh ;
As thou from year to year hast sung too late
    For my relief, yet hadst no reason why.
Whether the Muse or Love call thee his mate,
    Both them I serve, and of their train am I.
                 John Milton.

82. THE HOUR OF NIGHT

Now came still Evening on, and Twilight grey
    Had in her sober livery all things clad ;
Silence accompanied, for beast and bird,
They to their grassy couch, these to their nests
Were slunk, all but the wakeful nightingale ;
She all night long her amorous descant sung ;
Silence was pleased : now glow'd the firmament

With living sapphires : Hesperus, that led
The starry host, rode brightest, till the Moon,
Rising in clouded majesty, at length
Apparent queen, unveil'd her peerless light,
And o'er the dark her silver mantle threw.

John Milton.

83. MILTON (*Extract*)

O MIGHTY-MOUTH'D inventor of harmonies,
    O skill'd to sing of Time or Eternity,
God-gifted organ voice of England,
    Milton, a name to resound for ages.

Alfred, Lord Tennyson.

84. O SUMMER SUN, O MOVING TREES !

O SUMMER sun, O moving trees !
    O cheerful human noise, O busy glittering
        street !
What hour shall Fate in all the future find,
Or what delights ever to equal these !
Only to taste the warmth, the light, the wind,
Only to be alive, and feel that life is sweet ?

Laurence Binyon.

85. FOUR THINGS MAKE US HAPPY HERE

HEALTH is the first good lent to men ;
    A gentle disposition then :
Next, to be rich by no by-ways ;
Lastly, with friends t'enjoy our days.

Robert Herrick.

86. PRAYER FOR MICHAELMAS

GOOD Saint Michael, if we must
Leave our bodies here to dust,
Grant our souls a heaven where we
Still your Michaelmas may see.
Do not make me quire and sing
With radiant angels in a ring,
Nor idly tread a pearl-paved street
With my new, unearthly feet ;
Do not shut me in a heaven
Golden bright from morn to even,
Where no shadows and no showers
Dim the tedious, shining hours.
Grant that there be autumn still,
Smoke-blue dusk, blown crisp and chill ;
And let the furrowed plough-land bare
Curve strongly to the windswept air ;
Make the leafy beechwoods burn,
Russet, yellow, bronze by turn ;
And set the hedgerow and the briar
Thick with berries red as fire.
Let me search and gather up
Acorns green, with knobbled cup,
And prickly chestnuts, plumping down
To show a glossy kernel brown.
Splendid cities like me ill,
And for song I have no skill ;
Then let me, in an autumn wood,
Sweep, and pick up sticks for God.

Viola Gerard Garvin.

87. " NO ! "

No sun—no moon !
No morn—no noon—
No dawn—no dusk—no proper time of day—
No sky—no earthly view—
No distance looking blue—
No road—no street—no " t'other side the way "—
No end to any Row—
No indication where the Crescents go—
No top to any steeple—
No recognitions of familiar people—
No courtesies for showing 'em—
No knowing 'em !—
No travelling at all—no locomotion—
No inkling of the way—no notion—
" No go "—by land or ocean—
No mail—no post—
No news from any foreign coast—
No Park—no Ring—no afternoon gentility—
No company—no nobility—
No warmth, no cheerfulness, no healthful ease,
No comfortable feel in any member—
No shade, no shine, no butterflies, no bees,
No fruits, no flowers, no leaves, no birds—
No—vember !   *Thomas Hood.*

88. SONNET LXXIII

That time of year thou may'st in me behold
When yellow leaves, or none, or few, do hang
Upon those boughs which shake against the cold,
Bare ruin'd choirs, where late the sweet birds sang :

In me thou see'st the twilight of such day
As after sunset fadeth in the west,
Which by and by black night doth take away,
Death's second self, that seals up all in rest :
In me thou see'st the glowing of such fire
That on the ashes of his youth doth lie,
As the death-bed whereon it must expire,
Consumed with that which it was nourish'd by :

This thou perceiv'st, which makes thy love more
    strong,
To love that well which thou must leave ere long.
                                William Shakespeare.

89. NOËL

A FROSTY Christmas Eve
    when the stars were shining
Fared I forth alone
where westward falls the hill,
And from many a village
in the water'd valley
Distant music reach'd me,
peals of bells aringing :
The constellated sounds
ran sprinkling on earth's floor
As the dark vault above
with stars spangled o'er.

Then sped my thought to keep
that first Christmas of all
When the shepherds watching

7

by their folds ere the dawn
Heard music in the fields,
and marvelling could not tell
Whether it were angels
or the bright stars singing.

Now blessed be the tow'rs
That crown England so fair,
That stand up strong in prayer
unto God for our souls :
Blessed be their founders
(said I) an' our country folk
Who are ringing for Christ
in the belfries to-night,
With arms lifted to clutch
the rattling ropes that race
Into the dark above
and the mad romping din.

But to me heard afar
it was starry music
Angels' song, comforting
as the comfort of Christ,
When He spoke tenderly
to His sorrowful flock ;
The old words came to me
by the riches of time
Mellow'd and transfigured,
as I stood on the hill
Heark'ning in the aspect
of th' eternal silence.

Robert Bridges.

90. ODE ON THE MORNING OF CHRIST'S NATIVITY

THIS is the month, and this the happy morn
    Wherein the Son of Heaven's Eternal King,
Of wedded maid and virgin mother born,
Our great redemption from above did bring ;
For as the holy sages once did sing
That He our deadly forfeit should release,
And with His Father work us a perpetual peace.

That glorious Form, that light unsufferable,
And that far-beaming blaze of Majesty
Wherewith He wont at Heaven's high council-table
To sit the midst of Trinal Unity,
He laid aside ; and, here with us to be,
Forsook the courts of everlasting day,
And chose with us a darksome house of mortal clay.

Say, heavenly Muse, shall not thy sacred vein
Afford a present to the Infant God ?
Hast thou no verse, no hymn, or solemn strain
To welcome Him to this His new abode,
Now while the heaven, by the sun's team untrod,
Hath took no print of the approaching light,
And all the spangled host keep watch in squadrons
    bright ?

See how from far, upon the eastern road,
The star-led wizards haste with odours sweet :
O run, prevent them with thy humble ode
And lay it lowly at His blessed feet ;

Have thou the honour first thy Lord to greet,
And join thy voice unto the Angel quire
From out His secret altar touch'd with hallow'd fire.
John Milton.

91. THE ANGELS FOR THE NATIVITY OF OUR LORD

RUN, shepherds, run where Bethlem blest appears,
    We bring the best of news, be not dismayed,
A Saviour there is born, more old than years,
Amidst heaven's rolling heights this earth who
    stayed.
In a poor cottage inned, a virgin maid
A weakling did him bear, who all upbears ;
There is he poorly swaddl'd, in manger laid,
To whom too narrow swaddlings are our spheres :
Run, shepherds, run, and solemnize his birth,
This is that night—no ! day, grown great with bliss,
In which the power of Satan broken is ;
In heaven be glory, peace upon the earth !

Thus singing, through the air the angels swam,
And cope of stars re-echoéd the same.
William Drummond of Hawthornden.

92. ON THE HOLY NATIVITY OF OUR LORD GOD
(*Extract*)
THE HYMN

TITYRUS : GLOOMY night embraced the place
        Where the noble infant lay.
The Babe looked up and showed His face ;
In spite of darkness it was day.

It was Thy day, Sweet ! and did rise,
Not from the East, but from Thine eyes.

CHORUS : It was Thy day, Sweet ! and did rise,
Not from the East, but from Thine eyes.

THYRSIS : Winter chid aloud and sent
 The angry North to wage his wars.
The North forgot his fierce intent,
And left perfumes instead of scars.
By those sweet eyes' persuasive powers,
Where he meant frost he scattered flowers.

CHORUS : By those sweet eyes' persuasive powers,
Where he meant frost he scattered flowers.

BOTH : We saw thee in Thy Balmy nest,
 Young dawn of our eternal Day !
We saw Thine eyes break from the East,
And chase the trembling shades away.
We saw Thee ; and we blest the sight,
We saw Thee by Thine Own sweet light.

CHORUS : We saw Thee ; and we blest the sight,
We saw Thee by Thine Own sweet light.

TITYRUS : Poor world (said I), what wilt thou do
 To entertain this starry Stranger ?
Is this the best thou canst bestow ?
 A cold, and not too cleanly, manger ?
Contend the powers of Heaven and Earth,
To fit a bed for this huge birth.

CHORUS : Contend the powers of Heaven and
    Earth,
    To fit a bed for this huge birth.

THYRSIS : Proud world, said I, cease your contest,
    And let the mighty Babe alone.
The phœnix builds the phoenix' rest,
    Love's architecture is his own.
The Babe whose birth embraves this morn,
    Made His Own bed ere He was born.

CHORUS : The Babe whose birth embraves this
    morn,
    Made His Own bed ere He was born.

TITYRUS : I saw the curled drops, soft and slow,
    Come hovering o'er the place's head ;
Offering their whitest sheets of snow
    To furnish the fair Infant's bed ;
Forbear, said I, be not too bold,
    Your fleece is white, but 'tis too cold.

CHORUS : Forbear, said I, be not too bold,
    Your fleece is white, but 'tis too cold.

THYRSIS : I saw the obsequious Seraphim
    Their rosy fleece of fire bestow,
For well they now can spare their wings,
    Since Heaven itself lies here below.
Well done, said I ; but are you sure
Your down, so warm, will pass for pure ?

CHORUS : Well done, said I; but are you sure
Your down, so warm, will pass for pure ?

TITYRUS : No, no! your King's not yet to seek
   Where to repose His royal head ;
See, see, how soon his new-bloomed cheek
   'Twixt mother's breasts is gone to bed.
Sweet choice, said we ! no way but so
Not to lie cold, but sleep in snow.

CHORUS : Sweet choice, said we ! no way but so
Not to lie cold, but sleep in snow.

BOTH : To Thee, meet Majesty, soft King
   Of simple graces and sweet loves !
Each of us his lamb will bring,
   Each his pair of silver doves !
At last, in fire of Thy fair eyes,
Ourselves become our own best sacrifice !

CHORUS : At last, in fire of Thy fair eyes,
Ourselves become our own best sacrifice !
               Richard Crashaw.

93. THE HEAVENLY NOËL

OH ! what great thing is done to-night
   Or what good news has sped ?
What ails the blessed saints in Heaven,
   They cannot rest in bed ?
But up and down so ceaselessly
   They go in joy and dread.

The gate-house all is lighted up,
   Wherein Saint Peter dwells ;
St. James looks out of his great house,
   All made of oyster shells ;
In his good hostel by the flood
   St. Julian rings the bells.

St. Catherine wears her silver shoes
   And pearl-besprinkled gown ;
St. Barbara from her high, high tower
   Upon the earth looks down ;
Saint Christopher bends wondering eyes
   On David's distant town.

The Angels' chanting sounds afar
   An ancient waterfall ;
They do not listen to their strain,
   Nor answer to their call ;
Their thoughts are on the little earth,
   Not in the heavenly hall.

For there they see a lovelier thing
   Than is beyond the sky ;
They see the little Lord of Heaven
   Upon his hard bed lie ;
Their hearts are filled in wonder for
   The Change of the Most High.

Richard Lawson Gales.

94. A PASTORAL ON THE BIRTH OF OUR SAVIOUR
Betwixt
DAVID, THYRSIS, AND THE ANGEL GABRIEL

DAVID

WHAT means yon apparition in the sky,
     Thyrsis, that dazzles every shepherd's eye ?
I slumbering was when, from yon glorious cloud,
Came gliding music, heavenly sweet, and loud ;
With sacred raptures which my bosom fires,
And with celestial joy my soul inspires :
It soothes the native horrors of the night,
And gladdens nature more than dawning light.

THYRSIS

But hold ! see hither through the yielding air
An angel comes ! for mighty news prepare !

ANGEL GABRIEL

Rejoice, ye swains ! anticipate the morn
With songs of praise ; for lo, a Saviour's born !
With joyful haste to Bethlehem repair,
And you will find th' Almighty Infant there.
Wrapp'd in a swaddling band you'll find your King,
And in a manger laid : to Him your praises bring.

CHORUS OF ANGELS

To God who in the highest dwells,
    Immortal glory be :
Let peace be in the humble cells
    Of Adam's progeny.

DAVID

No more the year shall wintry horrors bring ;
Fix'd in th' indulgence of eternal Spring,
Immortal green shall clothe the hills and vales,
And odorous sweets shall load the balmy gales ;
The silver brooks shall in soft murmurs tell
The joy that shall their oozy channels swell.
Feed on, my flocks, and crop the tender grass ;
Let blooming joy appear on every face ;
For lo ! this blessed, this propitious morn,
The Saviour of lost mankind is born !

THYRSIS

Thou fairest morn that ever sprang from night,
Or deck'd the opening skies with rosy light !
Well may'st thou shine with a distinguished ray,
Since here Immanuel condescends to stay ;
Our fears, our guilt, our darkness to dispel,
And save us from the horrid jaws of hell ;
Who from His throne descended (matchless love !)
To guide poor mortals to bless'd seats above.
But come without delay, let us be gone :
Shepherd, let's go, and humbly kiss the Son.

James Thomson.

95. ST. AGNES' EVE

DEEP on the convent-roof the snows
    Are sparkling to the moon :
My breath to heaven like vapour goes :
    May my soul follow soon !

The shadows of the convent-towers
  Slant down the snowy sward,
Still creeping with the creeping hours
  That lead me to my Lord:
Make Thou my spirit pure and clear
  As are the frosty skies,
Or this first snowdrop of the year
  That in my bosom lies.

As these white robes are soiled and dark,
  To yonder shining ground;
As this pale taper's earthly spark,
  To yonder argent round;
So shows my soul before the Lamb,
  My spirit before Thee;
So in mine earthly house I am,
  To that I hope to be.
Break up the heavens, O Lord! and far,
  Thro' all yon starlight keen,
Draw me, Thy bride, a glittering star,
  In raiment white and clean.

He lifts me to the golden doors;
  The flashes come and go;
All heaven bursts her starry floors,
  And strows her lights below,
And deepens on and up; the gates
  Roll back, and far within
For me the Heavenly Bridegroom waits,
  To make me pure of sin.

The sabbaths of Eternity,
   One sabbath deep and wide—
A light upon the shining sea—
   The Bridegroom with His bride !
                    Alfred, Lord Tennyson.

96. SAN LORENZO GIUSTINIANI'S MOTHER

I HAD not seen my son's dear face
   (He chose the cloister by God's grace)
   Since it had come to full flower-time.
   I hardly guessed at its perfect prime,
That folded flower of his dear face.

Mine eyes were veiled by mists of tears
When on a day in many years
   One of his Order came.   I thrilled,
   Facing, I thought, that face fulfilled,
I doubted, for my mists of tears.

His blessing be with me for ever !
My hope and doubt were hard to sever.
   —That altered face, those holy weeds !
   I filled his wallet and kissed his beads,
And lost his echoing feet for ever.

If to my son my alms were given
I know not, and I wait for Heaven.
   He did not plead for child of mine,
   But for another Child divine,
And unto Him it was surely given.

There is One alone who cannot change ;
Dreams are we, shadows, visions strange ;

And all I give is given to One.
I might mistake my dearest son,
But never the Son who cannot change.
Alice Meynell.

97. SIR GALAHAD

MY good blade carves the casques of men,
  My tough lance thrusteth sure,
My strength is as the strength of ten
  Because my heart is pure.
The shattering trumpet shrilleth high,
  The hard brands shiver on the steel,
The splinter'd spear-shafts crack and fly,
  The horse and rider reel :
They reel, they roll in clanging lists,
  And when the tide of combat stands,
Perfume and flowers fall in showers,
  That lightly rain from ladies' hands.

How sweet are looks that ladies bend
  On whom their favours fall !
For them I battle till the end,
  To save from shame and thrall :
But all my heart is drawn above,
  My knees are bow'd in crypt and shrine :
I never felt the kiss of love,
  Nor maiden's hand in mine.
More bounteous aspects on me beam,
  Me mightier transports move and thrill ;
So I keep I fair thro' faith and prayer
  A virgin heart in work and will.

When down the stormy crescent goes,
　A light before me swims,
Between dark stems the forest glows,
　I hear a noise of hymns :
Then by some secret shrine I ride ;
　I hear a voice, but none are there ;
The stalls are void, the doors are wide,
　The tapers burning fair.
Fair gleams the snowy altar-cloth,
　The silver vessels sparkle clean,
The shrill bell rings, the censer swings,
　And solemn chaunts resound between.

Sometimes on lonely mountain-meres
　I find a magic bark ;
I leap on board : no helmsman steers :
　I float till all is dark.
A gentle sound, an awful light !
　Three angels bear the Holy Grail :
With folded feet, in stoles of white,
　On sleeping wings they sail.
Ah, blessed vision ! blood of God !
　My spirit beats her mortal bars,
As down dark tides the glory slides,
　And star-like mingles with the stars.

When on my goodly charger borne
　Thro' dreaming towns I go,
The cock crows ere the Christmas morn,
　The streets are dumb with snow.

The tempest crackles on the leads,
  And, ringing, spins from brand and mail
But o'er the dark a glory spreads,
  And gilds the driving hail.
I leave the plain, I climb the height ;
  No branchy thicket shelter yields ;
But blessed forms in whistling storms
  Fly o'er waste ferns and windy fields.

A maiden knight—to me is given
  Such hope, I know not fear ;
I yearn to breathe the airs of heaven
  That often meet me here.
I muse on joy that will not cease,
  Pure spaces clothed in living beams,
Pure lilies of eternal peace,
  Whose odours haunt my dreams ;
And, stricken by an angel's hand,
  This mortal armour that I wear,
This weight and size, this heart and eyes,
  Are touch'd, are turn'd, to finest air.

The clouds are broken in the sky,
  And thro' the mountain-walls
A rolling organ-harmony
  Swells up, and shakes and falls.
Then move the trees, the copses nod,
  Wings flutter, voices hover clear :
" O just the faithful knight of God !
  Ride on ! the prize is near."

So pass I hostel, hall, and grange ;
  By bridge and ford, by park and pale,
All-arm'd I ride, whate'er betide,
  Until I find the Holy Grail.
               Alfred, Lord Tennyson.

98. THE SOULS
In Cœlo Quies

Up from the field of Battle
  The souls of all the slain
Go sweeping up to Heaven's gate,
Through wind and storm and rain.

The roaring of the cannon
They now leave far behind,
The souls drift upward, one by one,
Like leaves before the wind.

They reach the shining portal,
And beat upon the door,
Oh, good Saint Peter, let us in,
For we can fight no more.

Saint Peter riseth from his seat,
He speaketh very slow,
Ere I can open wide the door,
Your passports ye must show.

No passports have we, wail the souls,
We died upon the field,
One moment quick, next moment dead,
For we would never yield.

Saint Peter mutters in his beard,
Ye died in mortal sin,
No penitence avails you now,
I cannot let you in.

But still the souls beat on the door,
And cry and cry again,
Till all the courts of heaven were stirred,
By reason of their pain.

On blessed Michael now they call,
Him with the shining sword,
Who standeth bright before the throne,
The Warrior of the Lord.

Oh, good Saint Michael, hear our plaint,
Thou wert a soldier, too,
We only did what we were told,
As soldiers have to do.

The Saint leaps down the golden stairs,
And shouts through all the din,
Good Brother, I must ope the gate,
To let my brethren in.

For they have fought the goodliest fight
That ever I heard tell,
Since when I bound the dragon's jaws,
And thrust him down to Hell.

Saint Michael opens wide the gate,
And bares his shining sword,
From henceforth till this war is done,
I'll keep both watch and ward.

The souls stream in with joyous cries,
Triumphantly they go,
Clad in gold armour passing bright,
The brazen trumpets blow.

And harps are struck, and people shout,
Whilst stern as unsheathed sword,
They stride along the golden streets,
The warriors of the Lord.

Saint Michael helps us in our need,
Of all dear Saints the best,
He giveth ease unto our souls,
And to our bodies rest.

Arthur Corder.

99. THE VOLUNTEER

HERE lies a clerk who half his life had spent
    Toiling at ledgers in a city grey,
Thinking that so his days would drift away
With no lance broken in life's tournament :
    Yet ever 'twixt the books and his bright eyes
The gleaming eagles of the legions came,
    And horsemen, charging under phantom skies,
Went thundering past beneath the oriflamme.

And now those waiting dreams are satisfied ;
  From twilight to the halls of dawn he went ;
  His lance is broken ; but he lies content
With that high hour, in which he lived and died.
  And falling thus, he wants no recompense,
Who found his battle in the last resort ;
  Nor needs he any hearse to bear him hence,
Who goes to join the men of Agincourt.

Herbert Asquith.

100. THE NOBLE NATURE

IT is not growing like a tree
  In bulk, doth make Man better be,
Or standing like an oak, three hundred year,
To fall a log at last, dry, bald, and sere :
    A lily of a day
    Is fairer far in May,
  Although it fall and die that night—
  It was the plant and flower of Light.
In small proportions we just beauties see ;
And in short measures life may perfect be.

Ben Jonson.

101. O YEARS !

O YEARS ! and Age ! Farewell :
  Behold I go,
  Where I do know
Infinity to dwell.

And these mine eyes shall see
  All times, how they
  Are lost i' th' Sea
Of vast Eternity.

Where never Moon shall sway
    The Stars ; but she,
    And Night, shall be
Drown'd in one endless Day.

Robert Herrick.

102. HEAVEN

O WHO will show me those delights on high ?
            Echo.   I.
Thou, Echo, thou art mortal, all men know.
            Echo.   No.
Wert thou not born among the trees and leaves ?
            Echo.   Leaves.
And are there any leaves that still abide ?
            Echo.   Bide.
What leaves are they ? impart the matter wholly.
            Echo.   Holy.
Are holy leaves the Echo, then, of bliss ?
            Echo.   Yes !
Then tell me, what is that supreme delight ?
            Echo.   Light.
Light to the mind : what shall the will enjoy ?
            Echo.   Joy.
But are there cares and business with the pleasure ?
            Echo.   Leisure.
Light, joy and leisure : but shall they perséver ?
            Echo.   Ever.

George Herbert.

103. SONNET

Not with vain tears, when we're beyond the sun,
   We'll beat on the substantial doors, nor
      tread
Those dusty high-roads of the aimless dead
Plaintive for Earth ; but rather turn and run
Down some close-covered by-way of the air,
   Some low sweet alley between wind and wind,
   Stoop under faint gleams, thread the shadows, find
Some whispering ghost-forgotten nook, and there

Spend in pure converse our eternal day ;
   Think each in each, immediately wise ;
Learn all we lacked before ; hear, know, and say
   What this tumultuous body now denies ;
And feel, who have laid our groping hands away ;
   And see, no longer blinded by our eyes.

                              Rupert Brooke.

104. PARADISE

I bless Thee, Lord, because I GROW
   Among Thy trees, which in a ROW,
To Thee both fruit and order OW.

What open force or hidden CHARM
Can blast my fruit, or bring me HARM,
While the enclosure is Thine ARM ?

Enclose me still for fear I START ;
Be to me rather sharp and TART
Than let me want Thy hand and ART :

When Thou dost greater judgments SPARE,
And with Thy knife but prune and PARE,
Ev'n fruitful trees more fruitful ARE :

Such sharpness shows the sweetest FRIEND,
Such cuttings rather heal than REND,
And such beginnings touch their END.

George Herbert.

105. TRUE LOVE (Sonnet CXVI)

LET me not to the marriage of true minds
   Admit impediments.   Love is not love
Which alters when it alteration finds,
Or bends with the remover to remove :—
O no ! it is an ever-fixéd mark
That looks on tempests, and is never shaken ;
It is the star to every wandering bark,
Whose worth's unknown, although his height be
   taken.
Love's not Time's fool, though rosy lips and cheeks
Within his bending sickle's compass come ;
Love alters not with his brief hours and weeks,
But bears it out ev'n to the edge of doom :—

If this be error, and upon me proved,
I never writ, nor no man ever loved.

William Shakespeare.

106. ORPHEUS

ORPHEUS with his lute made trees,
   And the mountain-tops that freeze,
  Bow themselves when he did sing :

To his music plants and flowers
Ever sprung, as sun and showers
   There had made a lasting spring.
Everything that heard him play,
Even the billows of the sea,
   Hung their heads, and then lay by.
In sweet music is such art,
Killing care and grief of heart
   Fall asleep, or hearing die.

               William Shakespeare.

107. EPITAPH ON SHAKESPEARE

WHAT needs my Shakespeare for his honoured
     bones
The labour of an age in piléd stones,
Or that his hallowed reliques should be hid
Under a star-ypointing pyramid ?
Dear son of memory, great heir of fame,
What need'st thou such weak witness of thy name ?
Thou, in our wonder and astonishment,
Hast built thyself a livelong monument.
For whilst, to the shame of slow-endeavouring art,
Thy easy numbers flow, and that each heart
Hath, from the leaves of thy unvalued book,
Those Delphic lines with deep impression took,
Then thou, our fancy of itself bereaving,
Dost make *us* marble with too much conceiving,
And so sepulchred in such pomp dost lie
That kings for such a tomb would wish to die.

               John Milton.

108. LIFE OF SHAKESPEARE

(1557)

'TWAS a tanner of Stratford called John,
   Who over to Wilmcote is gone :
" Come kiss me, sweet Mary ! "—
" John Shakespeare, how dare ye ? "—
" Faith, chuck, will ye wed me ? "—" Anon ! "

(1580)

There was an old knight, Thomas Lucy,
Who asked Master Will, why the deuce he
   Had ventured to bag
   That unfortunate stag ?—
Will replied, " I like venison, if juicy."

(1582)

There was an old couple of Shottery
Who exclaimed, " Isn't marriage a lottery ?
   For here is our Anne
   Gone and married a man
Who writes what we think is called Pottery."

(1585)

Said Will to himself, " I'm a lown ;
For Anne hath-a-way of her own,
   But i' faith 'tis no joke,
   This connubial yoke ;
So methinks I will run up to Town."

(1590)

In Town he consorted with men
Who lived by the use of the pen.
  Said Marlowe, " My friend
  Will Shakespeare's no end ;
We must look to our laurels, rare Ben ! "

(1608)

William said, " I am forty-and-four,
And London shall know me no more ;
  I'm a famous rich man,
  So I'll go back to Anne.—
Heaven send she's less shrewd than of yore ! "

(1616)

Now for all his misdeeds he atones,
Lying peacefully under the stones
  In the church by the Avon,
  Whereon is engraven :
' Be he cursed that moveth my bones.'

(For all Time)

So here's to the excellent John,
Who was truly a *sine quâ non* ;
  If a marrying whim
  Had *not* taken him,
The Avon had wanted her Swan !

[Note.—As for those who attribute to Bacon these Works, and leave
Shakespeare forsaken, *their* ' Advancement of Learning ' is most un-
discerning, and, needless to say, they're mistaken.]

Frank Sidgwick.

109. GULIELMUS REX

THE folk who lived in Shakespeare's day,
    And saw that gentle figure pass
By London Bridge, his frequent way—
They little knew what man he was.

The pointed beard, the courteous mien,
The equal port to high and low,
All this they saw or might have seen,—
But not the light behind the brow.

The doublet's modest grey or brown,
The slender sword-hilt's plain device,
What sign had these for prince or clown ?
Few turned, or none, to scan him twice.

Yet, 'twas the King of England's kings !
The rest with all their pomps and trains
Are mouldered, half-remembered things—
'Tis he alone who lives and reigns.

                    Thomas Bailey Aldrich.

110. SHAKESPEARE

OTHERS abide our question.   Thou art free.
    We ask and ask ; thou smilest and art still,
Out-topping knowledge.   For the loftiest hill
That to the stars uncrowns his majesty,
Planting his steadfast footsteps in the sea,
Making the heaven of heavens his dwelling-place,
Spares but the cloudy border of his base
To the foil'd searching of mortality :

And thou, who didst the stars and sunbeams know,
Self-school'd, self-scann'd, self-honour'd, self-secure,
Didst walk on earth unguessed at.   Better so !
All pains the immortal spirit must endure,
   All weakness that impairs, all griefs that bow,
   Find their sole voice in that victorious brow.
                     Matthew Arnold.

111. PHILOMELA

H<small>ARK</small> ! ah, the Nightingale !
   The tawny-throated !
Hark, from that moonlit cedar what a burst !
What triumph ! hark !—what pain !

O wanderer from a Grecian shore,
Still, after many years, in distant lands,
Still nourishing in thy bewildered brain
That wild, unquench'd deep-sunken, old-world pain—
Say, will it never heal ?
And can this fragrant lawn
With its cool trees, and night,
And the sweet, tranquil Thames,
And moonshine, and the dew,
To thy rack'd heart and brain
Afford no balm ?

Dost thou to-night behold,
Here, through the moonlight on this English grass,
The unfriendly palace in the Thracian wild ?
Dost thou again peruse
With hot cheeks and sear'd eyes
The too clear web, and thy dumb sister's shame ?

Dost thou once more assay
Thy flight, and feel come over thee,
Poor fugitive, the feathery change
Once more, and once more seem to make resound
With love and hate, triumph and agony,
Lone Daulis, and the high Cephissian Vale ?
Listen, Eugenia—
How thick the bursts come crowding through the
      leaves !
    Again—thou hearest !
    Eternal passion !
    Eternal pain !

                     Matthew Arnold.

112. ODE TO A NIGHTINGALE

My heart aches, and a drowsy numbness pains
    My sense, as though of hemlock I had drunk,
Or emptied some dull opiate to the drains
  One minute past, and Lethe-wards had sunk :
'Tis not through envy of thy happy lot,
  But being too happy in thine happiness,—
    That thou, light-wingéd Dryad of the trees,
      In some melodious plot
  Of beechen green, and shadows numberless,
    Singest of summer in full-throated ease.

O, for a draught of vintage, that hath been
  Cool'd a long age in the deep-delvéd earth,
Tasting of Flora and the country green,
    Dance, and Provençal song, and sunburnt mirth !

O for a beaker full of the warm South,
  Full of the true, the blushful Hippocrene,
    With beaded bubbles winking at the brim,
      And purple-stainéd mouth ;
That I might drink and leave the world unseen,
  And with thee fade away into the forest dim :

Fade far away, dissolve, and quite forget
  What thou among the leaves hast never known,
The weariness, the fever, and the fret
  Here, where men sit and hear each other groan ;
Where palsy shakes a few, sad, last gray hairs,
  Where youth grows pale, and spectre-thin, and dies
    Where but to think is to be full of sorrow
      And leaden-eyed despairs ;
  Where Beauty cannot keep her lustrous eyes,
    Or new Love pine at them beyond to-morrow.

Away ! away ! for I will fly to thee,
  Not charioted by Bacchus and his pards,
But on the viewless wings of Poesy,
  Though the dull brain perplexes and retards :
Already with thee ! tender is the night,
  And haply the Queen-Moon is on her throne,
    Cluster'd around by all her starry Fays ;
      But here there is no light,
  Save what from heaven is with the breezes blown
    Through verdurous glooms and winding mossy
    ways.

I cannot see what flowers are at my feet,
  Nor what soft incense hangs upon the boughs,
But, in embalméd darkness, guess each sweet
  Wherewith the seasonable month endows
The grass, the thicket, and the fruit-tree wild ;
    White hawthorn, and the pastoral eglantine ;
      Fast fading violets cover'd up in leaves ;
        And mid-May's eldest child,
  The coming musk-rose, full of dewy wine,
    The murmurous haunt of flies on summer eves.

Darkling I listen ; and for many a time
  I have been half in love with easeful Death,
Call'd him soft names in many a muséd rhyme,
  To take into the air my quiet breath ;
Now more than ever seems it rich to die,
  To cease upon the midnight with no pain,
    While thou art pouring forth thy soul abroad
      In such an ecstasy !
  Still wouldst thou sing, and I have ears in vain—
  To thy high requiem become a sod.

Thou wast not born for death, immortal Bird !
  No hungry generations tread thee down ;
The voice I hear this passing night was heard
  In ancient days by emperor and clown :
Perhaps the self-same song that found a path
  Through the sad heart of Ruth, when, sick for home,
    She stood in tears amid the alien corn ;
      The same that oft-times hath
  Charm'd magic casements, opening on the foam
  Of perilous seas, in faery lands forlorn.

Forlorn ! the very word is like a bell
  To toll me back from thee to my sole self !
Adieu ! the fancy cannot cheat so well
  As she is famed to do, deceiving elf.
Adieu ! adieu ! thy plaintive anthem fades
  Past the near meadows, over the still stream,
    Up the hill-side ; and now 'tis buried deep
      In the next valley-glades :
  Was it a vision, or a waking dream ?
    Fled is that music :—Do I wake or sleep ?

John Keats.

113. TO A SKYLARK

Hail to thee, blithe Spirit !
    Bird thou never wert,
That from heaven, or near it
    Pourest thy full heart
In profuse strains of unpremeditated art.

  Higher still and higher
    From the earth thou springest,
  Like a cloud of fire,
    The blue deep thou wingest,
And singing still dost soar, and soaring ever singest.

  In the golden lightning
    Of the sunken sun
  O'er which clouds are brightening,
    Thou dost float and run,
Like an unbodied joy whose race is just begun.

The pale purple even
   Melts around thy flight ;
Like a star of heaven
   In the broad daylight
Thou art unseen, but yet I hear thy shrill delight :

Keen as are the arrows
   Of that silver sphere,
Whose intense lamp narrows
   In the white dawn clear
Until we hardly see, we feel that it is there.

All the earth and air
   With thy voice is loud,
As, when night is bare,
   From one lonely cloud
The moon rains out her beams, and heaven is over-
      flow'd.

What thou art we know not ;
   What is most like thee ?
From rainbow clouds there flow not
   Drops so bright to see
As from thy presence showers a rain of melody ;—

Like a poet hidden
   In the light of thought,
Singing hymns unbidden,
   Till the world is wrought
To sympathy with hopes and fears it heeded not :

Like a high-born maiden
  In a palace tower,
Soothing her love-laden
  Soul in secret hour
With music sweet as love, which overflows her bower :

Like a glow-worm golden
  In a dell of dew,
Scattering unbeholden
  Its aerial hue
Among the flowers and grass, which screen it from the
    view :

Like a rose embower'd
  In its own green leaves,
By warm winds deflower'd,
  Till the scent it gives
Makes faint with too much sweet these heavy-wingéd
    thieves.

Sound of vernal showers
  On the twinkling grass,
Rain-awaken'd flowers,
  All that ever was
Joyous, and clear, and fresh, thy music doth surpass.

Teach us, sprite or bird,
  What sweet thoughts are thine :
I have never heard
  Praise of love or wine
That panted forth a flood of rapture so divine.
  9

Chorus hymeneal
    Or triumphal chaunt
Match'd with thine, would be all
    But an empty vaunt—
A thing wherein we feel there is some hidden want.

What objects are the fountains
    Of thy happy strain ?
What fields, or waves, or mountains ?
    What shapes of sky or plain ?
What love of thine own kind ? what ignorance of
        pain ?

With thy clear keen joyance
    Languor cannot be :
Shadow of annoyance
    Never came near thee :
Thou lovest ; but ne'er knew love's sad satiety.

Waking or asleep
    Thou of death must deem
Things more true and deep
    Than we mortals dream,
Or how could thy notes flow in such a crystal stream ?

We look before and after,
    And pine for what is not :
Our sincerest laughter
    With some pain is fraught ;
Our sweetest songs are those that tell of saddest
        thought.

Yet if we could scorn
   Hate, and pride, and fear ;
If we were things born
   Not to shed a tear,
I know not how thy joy we ever should come near.

Better than all measures
   Of delightful sound,
Better than all treasures
   That in books are found,
Thy skill to poet were, thou scorner of the ground !

Teach me half the gladness
   That thy brain must know,
Such harmonious madness
   From my lips would flow,
The world should listen then, as I am listening now !
              Percy Bysshe Shelley.

114. TO THE FIRST ZEPPELIN OVER LONDON
(In the measure of Shelley's " To a Skylark ")

HAIL to thee, high-flier,
   Who with generous heart
Pourest out thy fire
   Over earth's dim chart
In sundry spasms of well-premeditated art !

Like a monstrous bird
   Overseas thou comest ;
Melodies unheard
   Through the heavens thou hummest,
And bombing still dost soar, and soaring ever bombest.

O'er thy bloated carcass
   Plays the silver beam,
Where in azure dark, as
   In a nightmare dream,
Thy crew are swung and wish themselves elsewhere,
     I deem.

Forth from many a tile (hark !)
   Boom the happy guns,
Having quite a sky-lark
   Blazing at the Huns,
With now a decent shot, and now some rotten ones.

Didst thou look for panic,
   Counting on a scare
Caused by that Titanic
   Sausage up in air ?
Then let me tell thee, London hasn't turned a hair.

Calm she gazed with such eyes
   On the scene as though
Watching cokernut-shies
   Or a comet-show
Or pyrotechnics done by Messrs. Brock and Co.

Saw the last red light out,
   And, with jaunty tread,
After half a night out
   Struck for home and bed,
And on the usual pillow laid the usual head.

With the morrow's dawning
  Rose and, all serene,
Turned, a little yawning,
  To the day's routine,
And went about her work as if thou hadst not been.
Owen Seaman.

115. THE CHARGE OF THE LIGHT BRIGADE

HALF a league, half a league,
  Half a league onward,
All in the valley of Death
  Rode the six hundred.
" Forward, the Light Brigade !
Charge for the guns ! " he said :
Into the valley of Death
  Rode the six hundred.

" Forward, the Light Brigade ! "
Was there a man dismay'd ?
Not tho' the soldier knew
  Someone had blunder'd :
Theirs not to make reply,
Theirs not to reason why,
Theirs but to do and die :
Into the valley of Death
  Rode the six hundred.

Cannon to right of them,
Cannon to left of them,
Cannon in front of them
  Volley'd and thunder'd ;

Storm'd at with shot and shell,
Boldly they rode and well,
Into the jaws of Death,
Into the mouth of Hell
　Rode the six hundred.

Flash'd all their sabres bare,
Flash'd as they turn'd in air,
Sabring the gunners there,
Charging an army, while
　All the world wonder'd :
Plunged in the battery-smoke
Right thro' the line they broke ;
Cossack and Russian
Reel'd from the sabre-stroke
　Shatter'd and sunder'd.
Then they rode back, but not,
　Not the six hundred.

Cannon to right of them,
Cannon to left of them,
Cannon behind them
　Volley'd and thunder'd ;
Storm'd at with shot and shell,
While horse and hero fell,
They that had fought so well
Came thro' the jaws of Death
Back from the mouth of Hell,
All that was left of them,
　Left of six hundred.

When can their glory fade ?
O the wild charge they made !
　All the world wonder'd.
Honour the charge they made !
Honour the Light Brigade,
　Noble six hundred !

　　　　　Alfred, Lord Tennyson.

116. BARBARA FRIETCHIE

UP from the meadows rich with corn,
　Clear in the cool September morn,

The clustered spires of Frederick stand
Green-walled by the hills of Maryland.

Round about them orchards sweep,
Apple and peach tree fruited deep,

Fair as the garden of the Lord
To the eyes of the famished rebel horde,

On that pleasant morn of the early fall
When Lee marched over the mountain-wall ;

Over the mountains winding down,
Horse and foot, into Frederick town.

Forty flags with their silver stars,
Forty flags with their crimson bars,

Flapped in the morning wind ; the sun
Of noon looked down, and saw not one.

Up rose old Barbara Frietchie then,
Bowed with her fourscore years and ten ;

Bravest of all in Frederick town,
She took up the flag the men hauled down ;

In her attic window the staff she set,
To show that one heart was loyal yet.

Up the street came the rebel tread,
Stonewall Jackson riding ahead.

Under his slouched hat left and right
He glanced ; the old flag met his sight.

" Halt ! "—the dust-brown ranks stood fast.
" Fire ! "—out blazed the rifle-blast.

It shivered the window, pane and sash ;
It rent the banner with seam and gash.

Quick, as it fell from the broken staff,
Dame Barbara snatched the silken scarf.

She leaned far out on the window-sill,
And shook it forth with a royal will.

" Shoot, if you must, this old grey head,
But spare your country's flag," she said.

A shade of sadness, a blush of shame,
Over the face of the leader came ;

The nobler nature within him stirred
To life at that woman's deed and word :

" Who touches a hair of yon grey head
Dies like a dog !   March on ! " he said.

All day long through Frederick street
Sounded the tread of marching feet :

All day long that free flag tost
Over the heads of the rebel host.

Ever its torn folds rose and fell
On the loyal winds that loved it well ;

And through the hill-gaps sunset light
Shone over it with a warm good-night.

Barbara Frietchie's work is o'er,
And the Rebel rides on his raids no more.

Honour to her ! and let a tear
Fall, for her sake, on Stonewall's bier.

Over Barbara Frietchie's grave,
Flag of Freedom and Union, wave !

Peace and order and beauty draw
Round thy symbol of light and law ;

And ever the stars above look down
On thy stars below in Frederick town !

John Greenleaf Whittier.

117. MEG MERRILIES

OLD Meg she was a gipsy,
 And lived upon the moors ;
Her bed it was the brown heath turf,
 And her house was out of doors.
Her apples were swart blackberries,
 Her currants, pods o' broom ;
Her wine was dew of the wild white rose,
 Her book a churchyard tomb.

Her brothers were the craggy hills,
 Her sisters larchen trees ;
Alone with her great family
 She lived as she did please.
No breakfast had she many a morn,
 No dinner many a noon,
And, 'stead of supper, she would stare
 Full hard against the moon.

But every morn, of woodbine fresh
 She made her garlanding,
And, every night, the dark glen yew
 She wove, and she would sing.

And with her fingers old and brown,
   She plaited mats of rushes,
And gave them to the cottagers
   She met among the bushes.

Old Meg was brave as Margaret Queen,
   And tall as Amazon ;
An old red blanket cloak she wore,
   A chip-hat had she on ;
God rest her aged bones somewhere—
   She died full long agone !

                   John Keats.

118. ROBIN HOOD

No ! those days are gone away,
   And their hours are old and gray,
And their minutes buried all
Under the down-trodden pall
Of the leaves of many years :
Many times have Winter's shears,
Frozen North and chilling East,
Sounded tempests to the feast
Of the forest's whispering fleeces,
Since men knew nor rent nor leases.

   No, the bugle sounds no more,
And the twanging bow no more ;
Silent is the ivory shrill
Past the heath and up the hill ;

There is no mid-forest laugh,
Where lone Echo gives the half
To some wight, amaz'd to hear
Jesting, deep in forest drear.

On the fairest time of June
You may go, with sun or moon,
Or the seven stars to light you,
Or the polar ray to right you ;
But you never may behold
Little John or Robin bold ;
Never one, of all the clan,
Thrumming on an empty can
Some old hunting ditty, while
He doth his green way beguile
To fair hostess Merriment,
Down beside the pasture Trent ;
For he left the merry tale,
Messenger for spicy ale.

Gone, the merry morris din ;
Gone, the song of Gamelyn ;
Gone, the tough-belted outlaw,
Idling in the " grenë shawe " ;
All are gone away and past !
And if Robin should be cast
Sudden from his turfed grave,
And if Marian should have
Once again her forest days,
She would weep, and he would craze :
He would swear, for all his oaks,
Fallen beneath the dockyard strokes,

Have rotted on the briny seas ;
She would weep that her wild bees
Sang not to her—strange ! that honey
Can't be got without hard money !

So it is ; yet let us sing,
Honour to the old bow-string !
Honour to the bugle-horn !
Honour to the woods unshorn !
Honour to the Lincoln green !
Honour to the archer keen !
Honour to tight Little John,
And the horse he rode upon !
Honour to bold Robin Hood,
Sleeping in the underwood !
Honour to Maid Marian,
And to all the Sherwood clan !
Though their days have hurried by,
Let us two a burden try.

John Keats.

119. THE WIFE OF USHER'S WELL

THERE lived a wife at Usher's Well,
    And a wealthy wife was she :
She had three stout and stalwart sons
    And sent them o'er the sea.

They had not been a week from her,
    A week but barely ane,
When word came to the carline wife
    That her three sons were gane.

They had not been a week from her,
   A week but barely three,
When word came to the carline wife
   That her sons she'd never see.

" I wish the wind may never cease,
   Nor fishes in the flood,
Till my three sons come hame to me
   In earthly flesh and blood ! "

It fell about the Martinmas,
   When nights are lang and mirk,
The carline wife's three sons came hame,
   And their hats were of the birk.*

It neither grew in syke† nor ditch,
   Nor yet in ony sheugh,‡
But at the gates o' Paradise
   That birk grew fair eneugh.

" Blow up the fire, my maidens !
   Bring water from the well !
For all my house shall feast this night,
   Since my three sons are well ! "

And she has made to them a bed,
   She's made it large and wide ;
And she's ta'en her mantle her about ;
   Sat down at the bedside.

* Birch   † Marsh   ‡ Trench

Then up and crew the red, red cock,
   And up and crew the grey :
The eldest to the youngest said,
   " 'Tis time we were away ! "

The cock he hadna craw'd but ance,
   And clapp'd his wings at a',
When the youngest to the eldest said,
   " Brother, we must awa'.

" The cock doth craw, the day doth daw,
   The channerin' worm doth chide ;
Gin we be miss'd out o' our place,
   A sair pain we must bide."

" Lie still, lie still but a little wee while,
   Lie still but if we may ;
Gin my mother should miss us when she wakes,
   She'll go mad ere it be day."

"Fare ye well, my mother dear !
   Farewell to barn and byre !
And fare ye well, the bonny lass
   That kindles my mother's fire ! "

                     Old Ballad.

120. LIFE

LIFE ! I know not what thou art,
     But know that thou and I must part ;
And when, or how, or where we met,
I own to me 's a secret yet.

Life ! we have been long together
Through pleasant and through cloudy weather ;
'Tis hard to part when friends are dear—
Perhaps 'twill cost a sigh, a tear ;
—Then steal away, give little warning,
     Choose thine own time ;
Say not Good Night, but in some brighter clime
     Bid me Good Morning.

Anna Lætitia Barbauld.

121. THE DEMON LOVER

" O WHERE have you been, my long, long love,
     These seven long years and more ? "
" O, I'm come to seek my former vows
     Ye granted me before."

" Awa' wi' your former vows," she says,
     " For they will breed but strife ;
Awa' wi' your former vows," she says,
     " For I am become a wife.

" I am married to a ship's carpenter,
   A ship's carpenter he's bound ;
I wouldna he kenned my mind this night
   For twice five hundred pound."

He turned him right and round about
   And the tear blinded his e'e :
" I wad never hae trodden on Irish ground
   If it hadna been for thee.

" I might hae had a noble lady,
   Far, far beyond the sea ;
I might hae had a noble lady,
   Were it no' for the love o' thee."

" If ye might hae had a noble lady,
   Yoursel' ye had to blame ;
Ye might hae taken the noble lady,
   For ye kenned that I was nane."

" O fause are the vows o' womankind,
   But fair is their fause bodie :
I wad never hae trodden on Irish ground
   Were it no for the love o' thee."

" If I was to leave my husband dear
   And my wee young son also,
O what hae ye to take me to,
   If with you I should go ? "

10

" I hae seven ships upon the sea,
    The eighth brought me to land ;
With mariners and merchandise,
    And music on every hand.

" The ship wherein my love shall sail
    Is glorious to behold ;
The sails shall be o' the finest silk,
    And the masts o' beaten gowd."

She has taken up her wee young son,
    Kiss'd him baith cheek and chin :
" O fare ye well, my wee young son,
    For I'll never see you again ! "

She set her foot upon the ship,
    No mariners could she behold ;
But the sails were o' the taffetie,
    And the masts o' beaten gold.

She hadna sailed a league, a league,
    A league but barely twa,
Till she minded on her husband she left,
    And her wee young son alsua.

She had not sailed a league, a league,
    A league but barely three,
Till grim, grim grew his countenance,
    And drumlie grew his ee.

" O hold your tongue of your weeping," says he,
 " Of your weeping now let me be :
I'll show you where the white lilies grow
 On the banks o' Italie."

" O what hills are yon, yon pleasant hills,
 That the sun shines sweetly on ? "
" O yon are the hills o' Heaven," he said,
 " Where you will never won."

" O whaten-a mountain is yon," she said,
 " Sae dreary wi' frost and snow ? "
" O yon is the mountain o' Hell," he said,
 " Where you and I will go.

" But hold your tongue, my dearest dear,
 Let a' your follies a-be :
I'll show you where the white lilies grow,
 In the bottom o' the sea."

And aye as she turned her round about,
 Aye taller he seemed to be ;
Until that the tops o' that gallant ship
 Nae taller were than he.

He struck the top-mast wi' his hand,
 The fore-mast wi' his knee ;
And he brake that gallant ship in twain
 And sank her in the sea.

Old Ballad.

122. SAINT BRANDAN

SAINT BRANDAN sails the Northern Main :
    The brotherhoods of saints are glad.
He greets them once, he sails again :
So late !—such storms !—the Saint is mad !

He heard across the howling seas
Chime convent-bells on wintry nights ;
He saw on spray-swept Hebrides
Twinkle the monastery-lights ;

But north, still north, Saint Brandan steer'd :
And now no bells, no convents more !
The hurtling Polar lights are near'd ;
The sea without a human shore.

At last—(it was the Christmas night ;
Stars shone after a day of storm)—
He sees float past an iceberg white,
And on it—Christ !—a living form !

That furtive mien—that scowling eye—
Of hair that red and tufted fell—
It is—Oh, where shall Brandan fly ?—
The traitor Judas, out of Hell !

Palsied with terror, Brandan sate ;
The moon was bright, the iceberg near.
He hears a voice sigh humbly, " Wait !
By high permission I am here.

" One moment wait, thou holy man !
On earth my crime, my death they knew :
My name is under all men's ban :
Ah, tell them of my respite too !

" Tell them, one blessed Christmas night—
(It was the first after I came,
Breathing self-murder, frenzy, spite,
To rue my guilt in endless flame)—

" I felt, as I in torment lay
'Mid the souls plagued by heavenly power,
An angel touch mine arm and say—
' Go hence and cool thyself an hour ! '

" ' Ah, whence this mercy, Lord ? ' I said.
' The Leper recollect,' said He,
' Who ask'd the passers-by for aid,
In Joppa, and thy charity.'

" Then I remember'd how I went,
In Joppa, through the public street,
One morn, when the sirocco spent
Its storms of dust, with burning heat ;

" And in the street a Leper sate,
Shivering with fever, naked, old :
Sand raked his sores from heel to pate ;
The hot wind fever'd him five-fold.

" He gazed upon me as I pass'd,
And murmur'd, 'Help me, or I die!'
To the poor wretch my cloak I cast,
Saw him look eased, and hurried by.

" O Brandan! Think, what grace divine,
What blessing must true goodness shower,
If semblance of it faint, like mine,
Hath such inestimable power!

" Well-fed, well-clothed, well-friended, I
Did that chance act of good, that one;
Then went my way to kill and lie—
Forgot my good as soon as done.

" That germ of kindness, in the womb
Of Mercy caught, did not expire:
Outlives my guilt, outlives my doom,
And friends me in the pit of fire.

" Once every year, when carols wake,
On earth, the Christmas night's repose,
Arising from the sinners' lake,
I journey to these healing snows.

" I staunch with ice my burning breast,
With silence balm my whirling brain.
O Brandan! to this hour of rest,
That Joppan leper's ease was pain!"

Tears started to Saint Brandan's eyes :
He bow'd his head ; he breath'd a prayer.
When he look'd up—tenantless lies
The iceberg, in the frosty air !
Matthew Arnold.

123. THE RAVEN

ONCE upon a midnight dreary, while I pondered,
    weak and weary,
Over many a quaint and curious volume of forgotten
    lore,
While I nodded, nearly napping, suddenly there
    came a tapping
As of some one gently rapping, rapping at my chamber
    door.
" 'Tis some visitor," I mutter'd, " tapping at my
    chamber door—
        Only this and nothing more."

Ah, distinctly I remember it was in the bleak Decem-
    ber,
And each separate dying ember wrought its ghost
    upon the floor ;
Eagerly I wish'd the morrow ;   vainly had I sought
    to borrow
From my books surcease of sorrow, sorrow for the
    lost Lenore—
For the rare and radiant maiden whom the angels
    name Lenore—
        Nameless here for evermore.

And the silken sad uncertain rustling of each purple
  curtain
Thrill'd me—filled me with fantastic terrors never
  felt before ;
So that now to still the beating of my heart, I stood
  repeating,
" 'Tis some visitor entreating entrance at my chamber
  door—
Some late visitor entreating entrance at my chamber
  door ;
            This it is, and nothing more."

Presently my soul grew stronger ; hesitating then
  no longer,
" Sir," said I, " or madam, truly your forgiveness
  I implore ;
But the fact is I was napping, and so gently you came
  rapping,
And so faintly you came tapping, tapping at my
  chamber door,
That I scarce was sure I heard you " : here I open'd
  wide the door—
            Darkness there, and nothing more.

Deep into that darkness peering, long I stood there
  wondering, fearing,
Doubting, dreaming, dreams no mortal ever dared to
  dream before ;

But the silence was unbroken, and the darkness
    gave no token,
And the only word there spoken was the whisper'd
    word " Lenore ! "
This I whisper'd, and an echo murmur'd back the
    word " Lenore "—
        Merely this, and nothing more.

Back into the chamber turning, all my soul within
    me burning,
Soon I heard again a tapping somewhat louder than
    before,
" Surely," said I, " surely that is something at my
    window lattice ;
Let me see then what thereat is, and this mystery
    explore—
Let my heart be still a moment and this mystery
    explore ;
        'Tis the wind, and nothing more ! "

Open here I flung a shutter, when with many a
    flirt and flutter
In there stepp'd a stately raven of the saintly days
    of yore ;
Not the least obeisance made he ; not an instant
    stopp'd or stay'd he ;

But with mien of lord or lady, perch'd above my
 chamber door—
Perch'd upon a bust of Pallas, just above my chamber
 door—
  Perch'd and sat, and nothing more.

Then this ebony bird beguiling my sad fancy into
 smiling,
By the grave and stern decorum of the countenance
 it wore,
" Though thy crest be shorn and shaven, thou," I
 said, " art sure no craven,
Ghastly, grim, and ancient raven wandering from
 the nightly shore,
Tell me what thy lordly name is on the night's
 Plutonian shore " :
  Quoth the raven, " Nevermore ! "

Much I marvell'd this ungainly fowl to hear discourse
 so plainly,
Though its answer little meaning—little relevancy
 bore ;
For we cannot help agreeing that no living human
 being
Ever yet was blest with seeing bird above his chamber
 door,
Bird or beast upon the sculptur'd bust above his
 chamber door,
  With such a name as " Nevermore."

But the raven, sitting lonely on the placid bust,
spoke only
That one word, as if his soul in that one word he
did outpour ;
Nothing farther then he utter'd—not a feather then
he flutter'd—
Till I scarcely more than mutter'd, " Other friends
have flown before—
On the morrow he will leave me, as my hopes have
flown before."
      Then the bird said, " Nevermore."

Startled at the stillness broken by reply so aptly
spoken,
" Doubtless," said I, " what it utters is its only stock
and store,
Caught from some unhappy master whom unmerciful
disaster
Follow'd fast and follow'd faster, till his songs one
burden bore—
Till the dirges of his hope that melancholy burden
bore
      Of ' Never—nevermore.' "

But the raven still beguiling all my sad soul into
smiling,
Straight I wheel'd a cushion'd seat in front of bird,
and bust, and door ;
Then, upon the velvet sinking, I betook myself to
linking

Fancy unto fancy, thinking what this ominous bird
    of yore—
What this grim, ungainly, ghastly, gaunt and
    ominous bird of yore
        Meant in croaking " Nevermore."

This I sat engaged in guessing, but no syllable
    expressing
To the fowl whose fiery eyes now burnt into my
    bosom's core ;
This and more I sat divining, with my head at ease
    reclining
On the cushion's velvet lining that the lamp-light
    gloated o'er,
But whose violet velvet lining, with the lamp-light
    gloating o'er
        She shall press, ah, nevermore !

" Prophet ! " said I, " thing of evil—prophet still,
    if bird or devil !
By that heaven that bends above us, by that God
    we both adore—
Tell this soul, with sorrow laden, if within the distant
    Aidenn
It shall clasp a sainted maiden whom the angels
    name Lenore—
Clasp a rare and radiant maiden whom the angels
    name Lenore."
        Quoth the raven " Nevermore."

" Be that word our sign of parting, bird or fiend ! " I
 shriek'd, upstarting—
" Get thee back into the tempest and the night's
 Plutonian shore !
Leave no black plume as a token of the lie thy
 soul hath spoken !
Leave my loneliness unbroken, quit the bust above
 my door !
Take thy beak from out my heart and take thy
 form from off my door ! "
   Quoth the raven " Nevermore."

And the raven never flitting, still is sitting, still is
 sitting,
On the pallid bust of Pallas just above my chamber
 door ;
And his eyes have all the seeming of a dæmon's
 that is dreaming,
And the lamp-light o'er him streaming throws his
 shadow on the floor ;
And my soul from out that shadow that is floating
 on the floor
   Shall be lifted " Nevermore."
      Edgar Allan Poe.

124. A MUSICAL INSTRUMENT

WHAT was he doing, the great god Pan,
    Down in the reeds by the river ?
Spreading ruin and scattering ban,
    Splashing and paddling with hoof of a goat,
    And breaking the golden lilies afloat
      With the dragon-fly on the river.

He tore out a reed, the great god Pan,
    From the deep cool bed of the river :
The limpid water turbidly ran,
    And the broken lilies a-dying lay,
    And the dragon-fly had fled away,
      Ere he brought it out of the river.

High on the shore sate the great god Pan,
    While turbidly flowed the river ;
And hacked and hewed as a great god can,
    With his hard bleak steel at the patient reed,
    Till there was not a sign of a leaf indeed
      To prove it fresh from the river.

He cut it short, did the great god Pan
    (How tall it stood in the river !),
Then drew the pith, like the heart of a man,
    Steadily from the outside ring,
    And notched the poor dry empty thing
      In holes, as he sate by the river.

" This is the way," laughed the great god Pan
    (Laughed while he sate by the river),
" The only way, since gods began
    To make sweet music, they could succeed."
    Then, dropping his mouth to a hole in the reed,
    He blew in power by the river.

Sweet, sweet, sweet, O Pan !
    Piercing sweet by the river !
Blinding sweet, O great god Pan !
    The sun on the hill forgot to die,
    And the lilies revived, and the dragon-fly
    Came back to dream on the river.

Yet half a beast is the great god Pan,
    To laugh as he sits by the river,
Making a poet out of a man :
    The true gods sigh for the cost and pain,
    For the reed which grows nevermore again
    As a reed with the reeds in the river.

           Elizabeth Barrett Browning.

THE END

TO MY ILL-READER

THOU say'st my lines are hard,
  And I the truth will tell ;
They are both hard and marr'd,
  If thou not read'st them well.

Robert Herrick.

INDEX OF FIRST LINES